Suffering & God

Other Books by Alister E. McGrath . . .

ALISTER E. McGRATH

ZondervanPublishingHouse
Grand Rapids, Michigan

A Division of HarperCollinsPublishers

Suffering and God
Copyright © 1992, 1995 by Alister E. McGrath

Published by special arrangement with Hodder & Stoughton,
London. Published in the United Kingdom under the title *Suffering*.

Requests for information should be addressed to:
  Zondervan Publishing House
  Grand Rapids, Michigan 49530

Library of Congress Cataloging-in-Publication Data

McGrath, Alister E., 1953–
    Suffering and God / Alister E. McGrath.
        p.   cm.
    ISBN: 0–310–40691–9
    1. Suffering—Religious aspects—Christianity.   I. Title.
  BT732.7.M284   1995
  231'.8—dc 20   95–7344
                                                                                    CIP

Edited by Elizabeth Yoder

Printed in the United States of America

95 96 97 98 99 00 / ❖ DH / 10 9 8 7 6 5 4 3 2 1

CONTENTS

CONTENTS

Acknowledgments

ALTHOUGH THE ISSUES dealt with in this book have been on my mind for many years, I did not get around to writing it until July and August during an intensive month-long period of teaching at Ridley College, University of Melbourne, Australia. I am enormously grateful to Maurice and Jacqueline Betteridge, John and Lynn Pryor, and Bryden and Cathy Black for their hospitality and many kindnesses during my time in Australia. College secretaries Beryl Barter and Shirley Tongue cheerfully lent me their typewriters and made me coffee as I worked on the typescript of the work.

Introduction

I DECIDED TO WRITE this book shortly after a tutorial at Oxford University. I had assigned a student to write an essay on the problem of suffering. The reading list invited him to read and wrestle with the best of modern theology on the theme of suffering in relation to God. We met for our tutorial, but never got around to discussing the essay because he wanted to talk about something else. His father had just died, and he was devastated. He talked about how much he had loved his father and the deep sense of loss that his death evoked. He told me about his sense of sadness in knowing that his father would never know of his future life and career. He wondered what God might be saying to him through all this. Rather than discussing his essay, he was thinking out loud about the place of suffering in his own life and meditating on what he could learn through it. We talked for about an hour about the things that were on his mind.

Eventually, when I remembered that I was meant to be teaching him, not consoling him, I asked him if the reading for the essay I had assigned had been of any use to him in his situation. He smiled wryly and told me it had been something of a waste of time. "It all seemed so irrelevant," he said. Deep down, I knew what he meant. I could only agree that neat little explanations of suffering somehow seem very shallow in the face of the real thing.

That morning has remained in my memory ever since. It brought home to me how useless academic theology can be when one is faced with situations of real pastoral need. Somehow, for my student, theology seemed isolated from the distress and pain of his life. It was as if much of that writing on

9

suffering had no obvious relation to the pain and sorrow that ordinary Christians experience.

And yet theology is meant to be the servant of the church. It is supposed to enable the people of God to understand what is happening to them as they live out their faith in the world. It is intended to offer ordinary Christians a framework within which they may understand and cope with the tragedies and sorrows of their lives.

So I found myself, like my student, reflecting on suffering, thinking out loud about its presence and place in people's lives and especially in the lives of Christians. This little book is the result. It is a personal reflection on suffering, not a set of neat answers and pat solutions to the pain and bewilderment which suffering brings. All I have done is to approach my theme from a number of different angles, trying to open out its various aspects and make some kind of response to them. Nothing more. But if what is written here helps its readers in anything like the way that the thinking behind it has helped me, it will have been more than worthwhile.

ONE

The Balcony
and the Road

BROWSING IN PRINCETON'S Speer Library, with an hour or so
to spare before I was due to give some lectures, I came across
John Mackey's *Preface to Christian Theology*. It was not long
before I found myself held captive by a superb image Mackey
used to make one of his many memorable points. He entitled
the second chapter of his work "Two Perspectives: The Balcony
and the Road."

The imagery of the Balcony and the Road is drawn from
everyday life in the Spain of the 1920s, where Mackey had
spent a significant period of his life studying the Spanish language. He uses it to describe two very different ways of looking at the problems of life:

> By the Balcony . . . I mean that little platform in wood or stone
> that protrudes from the upper window of a Spanish home. There
> the family may gather of an evening to gaze spectator-wise upon
> the street beneath, or at the sunset or the stars beyond. . . . By the
> Road, I mean the place where life is tensely lived, where thought
> has its birth in conflict and concern, where choices are made and
> decisions are carried out. It is the place of action, of pilgrimage,
> of crusade, where concern is never absent from a wayfarer's
> heart. On the Road a goal is sought, dangers are faced, life is
> poured out. The two different perspectives are those of the spec-
> tator and of the participant. Those sitting comfortably on the

Balcony could watch those below them as they struggle in their journey, as they get lost on the Road, or as they try to work out what to do next. They need not get involved with their problems, except in a vaguely theoretical way.

Which of these two perspectives—the Balcony or the Road, the attitude of the observer or the participant—is the more important? Let us hear Mackey once more: "Truth is found upon the Road. It might even be said that only when a man descends from the Balcony to the Road, whether of his own free will, or because he has been pitched from it by providential circumstances, does he begin to know what reality is."

The true place of the Christian faith is on the Road. Those on the Road are facing real issues and have to make real decisions which will affect their future and their welfare. Those on the Road cannot know what lies over the brow of the next hill or what awaits them around the next bend. They are like people walking in the dark and on their own.

By contrast, those on the Balcony are spared the indecision and bewilderment so often experienced by those below them, who are wondering where the Road ahead of them leads and how likely they are to get to their intended destination. At its worst, the Balcony approach involves merely noticing other people suffering. It stimulates a convivial after-dinner discussion on where suffering comes from and a myriad of related academic issues which will occupy the diners for the remainder of a thought-provoking evening.

The problem, seen from the Road, is very different. Those on the Road are suffering and wondering how on earth they will cope with it and continue the life of faith as they suffer. They are participating in suffering, not observing it at a safe distance. Their difficulties are practical, not theoretical. They need something to help them keep going on that Road. The uncommitted and detached perspective of the Balcony seems to have little bearing on their position.

But it need not be like this. Those on the Balcony could be of help to those on the Road—above all, if they were fellow travelers engaged on the same journey. For at its best, the Balcony perspective can be profoundly helpful. Those on the Balcony can see further on account of their elevated position. Where those on the Road see only to the next bend, those on the Balcony can see where the Road is going and what it avoids. The Balcony provides a perspective to make sense of the Road.

High above the Road, those on the Balcony overhear the questions being asked by the travelers. They could, if they want to, come down from the Balcony and be of some use to those on the Road. They could tell them of what they see beyond the brow of the hill. They could assure them that others trudging along that Road have asked more or less the same questions and worried about the same things. They could share with them the collected wisdom of past travelers, making the discoveries of that past available to those who need them in the present. In short, they could make the lot of those travelers much easier.

Just as the Balconeers overhear conversations from below on the Road, so the theologian can explain how Christians from the earliest of times to the present have wrestled with the problem of suffering. John of Salisbury, a great writer of the Middle Ages, suggested that theologians are like "dwarves sitting on the shoulders of giants." They are able to see more and see further, not on account of their own greatness, but because of the stature of those upon whose shoulders they sit. To stand on that Balcony is to stand on the shoulders of generation after generation of Christian thinkers who have wrestled with these problems. There is no need to begin all over again, for we can make them our starting point.

The theologian can allow believers of today to overhear the conversations of the past that cast light on the purpose and place of suffering in the Christian life. As the great Swiss theologian Karl Barth wrote,

> We cannot be in the church without taking as much responsibility for the theology of the past as for the theology of the present.

Augustine, Thomas Aquinas, Luther, Schleiermacher and all the rest are not dead but living. They still speak and demand a hearing as living voices, as surely as we know that they and we belong together in the church.

Just as the Balconeers had a different perspective from those on the Road, so the theologian allows suffering to be seen from a different vantage point. He or she will try to place it in the context of the overall purposes of God for believers. Although the Balcony can easily become an ivory tower, a way of escaping from the world, as Martin Luther pointed out, it need not, and should not be so. The true theologian is one who suffers with the people of God and who tries to make sense of this suffering within the purposes and providence of God. Sharing that suffering, the theologian aims to gain a true perspective upon it, asking how it might be seen in a fresh light or harnessed to bring about spiritual maturity.

Those who are struggling with the life of faith need to be consoled and reassured. Yet the consolation offered must be genuine. It must be based on the bedrock of Christian truth, not on the white lies of well-meant deception. Given that suffering happens, what can be said to those passing beneath its shadow? What consolation can be offered to them?

Theology may not be able to abolish suffering, but it can allow that suffering to be seen in a new light. Although the way things are cannot be changed, the way in which people view them and respond to them can. The theologian can reassure believers of the validity of their faith and help them to apply it to the riddles of life, for faith makes a vital difference to the way we see and experience things. Just as the sun shines upon both the righteous and the unrighteous, so both the believer and the nonbeliever suffer and die. The vital difference lies in the way in which they experience and understand what is happening to them.

As we shall see, the gospel allows us to think positively about suffering. The theologian can explain how this works and reassure believers that to think positively about suffering is not to take refuge in unreality. The Christian's outlook on suffering is grounded in the self-revelation of God, and is not the product of despairing human imagination.

And finally, the theologian can reassure us that the Christian approach to suffering is true. How can we know that it is not just some consoling philosophy dreamed up by idealists who live in a make-believe world? There seems to be something within human nature which makes us trust things in inverse proportion to their value. The more someone offers to give us, the less likely we are to believe him or her. "There must be a catch somewhere!" The theologian can help by reassuring those on the Road that their hope in the face of suffering and pain is for real, that it is grounded in the real life, death, and resurrection of Jesus Christ.

Suffering is a pastoral and spiritual issue, not just a theological problem. In this book I have not the slightest intention of presenting myself either as a spokesman or as some kind of defense attorney for God. God is perfectly capable of looking after himself. The real issue is not about defending God's honor or integrity, but about making sense of our experience. How can we relate God to our world of suffering? It is our grasp of the situation that is so often at fault and that needs to be explored. As I hope to show, taking the trouble to relate the depths of Christian thought (the Balcony) to our experience of suffering (the Road) can give us a fresh perspective which will transform and mature us.

For being a Christian does not mean avoiding suffering, as if God calls believers out of this world into a cozy Christian environment from which difficulties are banished. No. Believers are called to remain in the world, sharing its pain, and working to transform it from within. The cross of Christ stands as a solemn and powerful reminder that God himself was prepared to suffer in order to redeem the world, and that God expects his people to share the same commitment and pain as they participate in the task of restoring a fallen world to its former glory. At the root of the Christian attitude to suffering is a passionate belief that our experience of suffering can, by the grace of God, be converted into something positive, something which makes us better and more caring individuals and communities. Seen in the right manner and offered to God for his gentle, healing touch, suffering can be transfigured into something glorious, which draws us closer to God and hints of that final time in the new Jerusalem when suffering will be nothing more than a memory.

TWO

Blaming God

In *THE BROTHERS KARAMAZOV*, the great nineteenth-century Russian novelist Fyodor Dostoyevsky tells of a harrowing incident in which an autocratic Russian ruler sets a pack of dogs upon an unfortunate child who is torn to pieces. Ivan Karamazov, one of the central characters of the novel, registers a powerful protest against this action. He declares that he is going to hand God back his ticket.

As Karl Marx once wrote, "the important thing is not to understand the world, but to change it." If Marx is right, theories about suffering cut no ice unless they allow us to abolish it. In a Marxist's eyes, Karamazov's protest is utterly futile. He may hand God back his ticket, but what does that accomplish? He makes some kind of moral statement, but does it stop suffering in the world?

When I was a teenager, I was strongly attracted to Marxism. Like many of my contemporaries, I saw it as the answer to society's suffering and injustice. I was an idealist, and, like many young people, I was entranced by ideals which I thought could be realized. Marxism appealed to that idealism and fueled it. It seemed to have the answer to suffering. Suffering was the result of the inhuman social conditions, faulty economics, and the political corruption of capitalism. Abolish capitalism, and the ills of the world would cease. When the revolution came, suffering would finally end and a new era in the history of the human race would dawn.

The recent experience of the Soviet Union and other militantly atheist states suggests that abandoning faith in God, far from liberating humanity from suffering, actually creates far more. Still, it would be wrong to accuse Marxism of being especially naive or misguided. Modern Western culture also fosters the illusion of being able to overcome suffering. We were informed that better education would eliminate the causes of suffering, yet nothing of the sort has happened. We were confidently told that better medical care would alleviate human suffering, but the root causes of suffering, which the medical profession can at best reduce by skilled use of pain-killing drugs, remain. In short, the Western liberal dream hoped that social evolution would lead to the elimination of human misery through the dawn of a brave new world. But paradise seems to have been postponed yet again.

Many people seem unable to cope with this harsh reality. Instead of acknowledging that there seems to be something wrong with human nature causing people to inflict suffering on others, they have taken the easy way out, blaming God for all the ills of the world. Many Jews became atheists as a result of the events that took place in the Second World War, especially in the extermination camps. But it wasn't God who engineered the Holocaust; it was human beings. It wasn't God who developed the atom bomb nor who dropped it on Hiroshima. It wasn't God who directed the liquidation squads during Stalin's purges. It was sinful and fallen human beings. This dreadful truth shatters the shallow and facile optimism of liberalism, which insists in the most doctrinaire manner upon the basic goodness of humanity, and ignores humanity's darker side.

"The scum and glory of the universe" was Pascal's judgment on human nature. Capable of soaring to tremendous artistic, cultural, and moral heights, we are just as prone to sink to the most appalling depths. Trying to pin the blame on God is a crude evasion of human responsibility; it is as unfair as it is unrealistic. A more helpful approach is to ask the following questions: Why do we get angry with God when people suffer? Why are we so distressed when someone we love suffers and dies?

Our sense of loss and sorrow when someone dies is in direct proportion to how much we love him or her. Our heartache would cease if we cared nothing for others and regarded everyone with a splendid sense of detachment. Like the Stoics of old, we could then remain unaffected by the suffering and death of those around us. As a philosophy of life, this seems to have much in its favor (unless, of course, we must suffer ourselves). But the price paid is astonishingly high—too high for any normal human being to take it seriously—because it involves sacrificing one of the most basic aspects of human nature: love and concern for others. There is something about human nature which makes us want to care for others and to be cared for by them. As Tennyson wrote in the famous lines from "In Memoriam":

> 'Tis better to have loved and lost
> Than never to have loved at all.

We suffer when those whom we love suffer. Love is the link which unites us with the lives of others and allows the pain of their suffering to spill over into our lives. There is a bittersweet bond between love and suffering—a bond which the Cross itself, as we shall see, both demonstrates and strengthens.

Jesus wept for his friend Lazarus, and those who were witness to those tears realized what they meant. "See how he loved him" (John 11:36). Love united Christ and Lazarus, moving Jesus to tears on account of Lazarus's plight. The gospel demands that we should love one another and bear one another's burdens. Yet the more we love others, the more we are moved and saddened by their suffering. The command to love is a command to share in the sufferings of others.

This insight is vital to any responsible Christian approach to suffering. For just as we are moved by the sufferings of those whom we love, so God is moved by the pain and sorrow of those whom he loves. For the Christian, the extent of the love of God is not in doubt: the Son of God died in order that we might know its full depths. It is not as if God is unaffected by our suffering. Just as Christ wept over the dead Lazarus, so our compassionate God weeps alongside us as we mourn for our friends, suffer, and die. The pages of history are stained by the tears of our God, who is working to bring about the day when "There will be no more death or mourning or crying or pain" (Rev. 21:4).

But this naturally raises the following question: Why doesn't God end suffering now?

THREE

God Almighty?

I‍F GOD CAN do anything, why doesn't he put an end to suffering? If God is omnipotent, why can't he decree that suffering will be abolished? Those sorts of thoughts have gone through my mind many times. Just about everyone asks questions like these at some time in their lives. It is not the originality but the familiarity of the question that obliges Christians to give some kind of answer.

The problem could be summed up like this. God is omnipotent. The meaning of that is simple: God can do anything he chooses. Of course, we have to make allowance for the logicians, who, feeling piqued at being left out of most theological discussions, want to get a word in edgeways here. "God can't make a square circle! He would contradict himself if he did." The logic of this is undeniable. Squares and circles are both shapes. They are different shapes. So a single shape cannot be both a square and a circle. God could make a circle or a square, but not a square circle. We may store this point in our memory in the hope that it might, for once, be useful, but the real problem lies elsewhere.

The real problem is that we are not critical enough in our thinking about God. We tend to think we already know exactly what God is like. We don't need to be told anything about him. So we happily begin our speculation with God's omnipotence. God can do anything. If he couldn't, he wouldn't be God, would he? But where does this idea actually come from? Does it fit in with a Christian understanding of God? We need to inquire very carefully about what Christianity actually says about God. By doing so, we might well end up challenging much popular thinking about lots of things, including the problem of suffering. So let's begin to explore our question with this point in mind.

Can God really do anything? Could he command someone to hate him, for example? There is no logical contradiction here, but there still seems to be something terribly wrong. Although there is no contradiction within the statement itself, it seems to fly in the face of everything we know about God. It is not logic, but basic Christianity, which is offended. The problem is not internal (with the logic), but external (with the view of God it implies). Let's try another example.

Could God prevent every human being that has ever turned to him in faith from being saved? No square circles lurking in the background there. At the logical level, there is no difficulty in declaring that God, being omnipotent, could deny salvation to everyone that has ever trusted in him. But again, basic Christian faith is outraged. For deep down, we know that God just isn't like that. The God that we know and love has promised in Scripture to save people who put their trust in him. If God were to deny them all salvation, he would contradict everything that we know about him; he would be breaking his promise. The logician would immediately reply that there is no logical contradiction in breaking a promise. People do it all the time. Why should being all-powerful stop anyone from breaking promises? Being omnipotent is about power, not morality.

But this little skirmish into the realms of theological fancy has exposed an important and neglected aspect of the problem of suffering. The simple fact of the matter is that God is *not* now able to do everything. God's hands are tied. He has made promises—promises which limit his freedom of action. God is faithful to his promises, and those promises are not arbitrary. They reflect and rest upon God's unchanging character; they tell us about the way God is. They express his consistency and faithfulness, as well as offer us salvation. What God *promises* expresses what God *is*.

Some further exploration is in order. Let us try to imagine God in eternity, before the creation of the universe as we know it. What sort of options might he have had? Two obvious ones might be:

1. To create a universe.
2. Not to create a universe.

God is perfectly free to choose either of these possibilities. Now notice that they are mutually exclusive. Doing one means not doing the other. God cannot do them both—not because of any weakness or inability on his part, but simply because we are talking about an utter absurdity. The statement *God can create the universe and at the same time not create the universe* is simply a meaningless combination of words, which does not suddenly make sense just because the word *God* is slipped in at its beginning. (Maybe logic has its uses after all!)

But what happens when one of these possibilities is actualized? Suppose God were to decide to create a universe. (As Christianity teaches, this decision was not forced upon God, but was chosen by him, in accordance with his unchanging character. It expressed his nature and purpose.) So God duly brings a universe into being. Could he will this universe to cease to exist, simply because he changes his mind?

No. God's decision to create a universe is not arbitrary or negotiable. God's decisions express God's nature. Furthermore, God's nature is unchanging. He is consistent in what he is, and thus in what he does. Once God acts, he is bound by his actions. He has made a decision. He has imposed limitations upon his own freedom for action.

Again, consider two quite different possibilities open to God in eternity before the founding of the world:

1. To offer salvation to all those who repent and turn to him.

2. To deny salvation to all those who repent and turn
   to him.
   (Note that there is no logical difficulty with either
   of these options.)

The Bible affirms that God selected the first of these two
options. Everything we know about God through Christ and in
Scripture points unhesitatingly towards this fact. But could
God change his mind? Could he now declare that the rules of
the game have been changed, and that from this moment
onward, salvation will be withheld from all those who repent
and turn to him?

No. A promise rests upon the faithfulness of the one who
promises. It expresses both the content of that promise (what is
being offered to us) and the trustworthiness of the one who
offers it to us. God has promised to act in a certain way. He has
established a definite process of salvation, which will apply
until the end of history. God will not go back on the promises
sealed and declared in his Son, Jesus Christ.

God is faithful and reliable, and for that very reason he
cannot be omnipotent. This might seem a strange thing to suggest; however, a little reflection will show that it is true. To be
reliable means that you do not—and more than that, you cannot—break a promise. It means that you cannot arbitrarily
change your mind. Take two statements like this:

1. God can change his mind about things and need
   not be restricted by what he promised in the past.
2. God is faithful to his promises.

At the logical level, these statements are both perfectly
acceptable. But the logician will immediately add a vital point:
they cannot both be true at the same time. If the first is true, the
second is false and vice versa. The theologian will then insist
that it is the second which is true. If God is totally omnipotent,
then no options are closed off to him, except those which are
logically impossible. But the simple fact is that the God whom
Christians know and worship, and who makes himself known

in and through Jesus Christ, is steadfast, constant, and faithful. And thus God cannot do anything; his options are restricted because he has chosen to restrict them.

The great theologians of the later Middle Ages, such as William of Ockham, were perfectly familiar with the point at issue here. In his famous discussion of the opening line of the Apostles' Creed—"I believe in God the Father almighty"— Ockham immediately asks precisely what is meant by that deceptively simple word *almighty*. It cannot, he argues, mean that God is presently able to do everything, although it does mean that God was once free to act in this way. God has established an order of things that reflects his loving and righteous will; and that order, once established, will remain until the end of time.

Ockham uses two terms to refer to these different options. The *absolute* power of God refers to God's options before he had committed himself to any course of action or world ordering. The *ordained* power of God refers to the way things are, which reflects the will of God their creator. These do not represent two different sets of options now open to God. They represent two different moments in the history of human salvation. Our concern is with the ordained power of God, the way in which God orders his creation at present.

For Ockham, God cannot now do everything. He has deliberately limited his possibilities. In his omnipotence, God chose to limit his own options. Is that a contradiction? No. If God is really capable of doing anything, he must be able to commit himself to a course of action and stay committed to it. Otherwise, there is something which God cannot do, thus calling into question his omnipotence. Ockham's approach, though long neglected, needs to be recovered and valued; for it represents a responsible, helpful, and thoroughly Christian approach to the question of God's omnipotence.

Another way of thinking focuses on the idea of the covenant between God and his people. "'This is the covenant I will make with the house of Israel after that time,' declares the LORD. 'I will put my law in their minds and write it on their hearts. I will be their God, and they will be my people'" (Jer. 31:33). This represents both a promise and a commitment. Can God now break this promise? Can he renege on this commitment? No. That would involve God's behaving in a way that is inconsistent with his very nature. Having promised, God keeps his word. God's options are limited by his promises on the one hand, and by his faithful nature on the other. He is no longer able to do everything.

So where does this leave all the abstract talk about God being omnipotent? In something of a state of ruin, is the short answer. The neat simplifications of the philosophers are left in tatters. God is indeed almighty, but that does not mean that he can do anything and everything. God's choices are limited, not from any weakness or failure on his part, but from a decision to deliberately restrict his own options. It is a self-imposed limitation. Only God had the right and the ability to limit his own course of action.

So what bearing do these thoughts have on human suffering? First, let us note the way in which God is affected by suffering. A totally omnipotent god could have avoided being affected in any way by the sorrow and grief of the world. But "the God of the Christians" (Tertullian)—the God that we are talking about—is pained by the suffering of the world. His very nature leads him to decide that he will enter into it, as one of us, in the person of his Son, Jesus Christ. In his love for us, he bears our sorrows and is acquainted with our grief.

We need to let this point sink in. God decided to be hurt by our pain. God allowed himself to suffer as we suffer and to share in our grief. Just as Jesus wept over the tomb of his friend Lazarus, so God is moved by our sadness. The Cross is the supreme demonstration of God's solidarity with us in this world of suffering. He chose to enter this world and to share its sorrow and pain. And he chose, finally, to suffer death on a cross, not because he had to, as if he was under some kind of external pressure to do so, but because he *wanted* to.

FOUR

A Loving God?

IF GOD IS so loving, why does he allow suffering? For many people the fact of suffering calls into question the goodness of God, since suffering and love seem to be mutually exclusive. The argument leading to this conclusion is usually set out like this:

1. God is almighty.
2. God is completely loving.
3. There is suffering and evil in the world.

A fourth idea has to be added before there is a logical problem. There is a logical contradiction if either:

1. An almighty and loving God could eliminate suffering entirely, or,
2. There are no good reasons for God to allow suffering.

If either or both of these could be shown to be right, a serious problem with the Christian view of God might well have been exposed. But neither has been shown to be true.

Let us take the second of these two statements first. Are there no good reasons for God's permitting suffering? We know that pain serves the vital biological function of alerting us to injury and the need for treatment. It serves to warn us of danger. In the same way suffering serves a vital *spiritual* function.

It reminds us of our mortality, preventing us from entertaining delusions about our nature and our future.

But some would reply that a world in which there is suffering cannot be a good world. Surely God could have created a better world? If this is the kind of world that God created, he can't be up to much. Such critics are putting themselves in the position of declaring that they know a better world must be possible, an approach that was devastatingly criticized by David Hume in the eighteenth century. Writing against those who claimed that this world was "the best of all possible worlds," Hume stressed that we know only this world. We have nothing else to compare it with.

The real problem does not lie at the level of logic, however, but in our intuitive feeling that a loving God could not allow suffering. Somehow we seem to imagine that suffering is the direct opposite of love, so that the Christian belief in a loving God is inconsistent with the presence of suffering in the world. Yet in reality, love and suffering are not necessarily opposed at all. Indeed they often stand together, almost as if they were two sides of the same coin.

The suffering of the Son of God is the most urgent and persuasive demonstration of the amazing extent to which God loves us. Where some suggest that love should abolish suffering, or that love can only be expressed in a world without pain, the gospel knows of a love that makes itself known in and through the suffering of Christ. This insight seems to me to be not merely astonishing; it holds the key to new ways of coping with the grim reality of suffering. The ancient Stoics taught us to suffer with dignity; Christ allows us to suffer in hope.

But how can suffering and love coexist in God? An objection might go like this: "If God is really loving, he would want us all to be happy. But we suffer, and we are not happy when we suffer. Therefore God cannot be loving." But what sort of idea of happiness is involved here? What sort of happiness are we meant to pursue?

A Loving God?

The idea of *happiness* is all too often used in a trivial way, as if the individual were the center and measure of all things. If I were phenomenally wealthy, I would be happy. Or would I? Would I not sleep uneasily, beset by a whole new range of problems, moral and practical, arising from the possession of wealth? How would I keep it? I might be a target for kidnappers, extortionists, and the tax authorities. And what of those others who are poor in order that I can be rich? I might well dream of a paradise in which I was totally happy, with all my needs and cares being taken care of by others. But what of those others?

What of the slaves who made the planters of the Deep South happy? What of the underpaid and undernourished workers of the Third World, who provide the goods that make me cozy and happy? What is the cost of my self-centered and happy world? My happiness is purchased through the suffering of others. Paradoxically, it is only by studiously ignoring the social cost of individual happiness that I can maintain that illusion of happiness. Being aware of the price paid for this personal gratification makes us develop a social conscience which willingly sacrifices individual happiness in order to promote the common good.

So could we really believe in a god who just pampers individuals, making them happy? And can we really equate *love* with "making us feel good"? Only love in the shallowest sense of the word would content itself with indulging the appetites, ambitions, and vices of individual humans. But this is not what the love of God is like. We must do God the basic justice of allowing his idea of love to be heard. We need to be taught what love, in the fully Christian sense of the word, actually means. We do not know; we need to learn.

The love of God is not some kind of indulgent benevolence which smiles upon our whims without asking whether they are innocent or profoundly destructive, and then generously allows us to have what we want. It involves our transformation. It involves our reshaping, so that we may desire and receive those things which are, in the mind of God our creator, for our greatest good. God has created us; we must listen to our maker concerning what is best for us. Precisely because of God's astonishing and overwhelming love for us, shown through the death of Christ upon the cross, he wants us to have nothing but the best. And what could be better than fellowship with God—something which nothing can ever destroy? George Herbert makes this point superbly in his poem "Love."

> Love bade me welcome; yet my soul drew back,
> Guilty of dust and sin.
> But quick-eyed Love, observing me grow slack
> From my first entrance in,
> Drew nearer to me, sweetly questioning
> If I lacked anything.
> "A guest," I answered, "worthy to be here."
> Love said, "You shall be he."
> "I, the unkind, ungrateful? Ah, my dear,
> I cannot look on thee."
> Love took my hand, and smiling did reply,
> "Who made the eyes but I?"
>
> "Truth, Lord, but I have marred them; let my shame
> Go where it doth deserve."
> "And know you not," says Love, "who bore the blame?"
> "My dear, then I will serve."
> "You must sit down," says Love, "and taste my meat."
> So I did sit and eat.

But this, some will object, is pure paternalism, even if it is also splendid poetry. It seems absurd to look to God to tell us what is best for us. It seems even more absurd to suggest that God meets all our needs and hopes. This seems simply childish nonsense in an age in which humanity has grown up.

Initially this objection might seem to have some weight, but not for long. A survey of the monuments to recent major human decisions concerning what is best for our race hardly makes inspiring reading: the First World War, the gas chambers of Auschwitz, the atom bomb of Hiroshima, the killing fields of Cambodia. The list goes on. It is a terrifying monument to what happens when humans start acting as if they are God. It testifies to the unreliability of human notions of what is right. Hitler thought he knew what was best for the German people. That vision happened to involve the extermination of millions of people. Stalin had no doubts about what was best for the Soviet Union. That vision happened to involve the liquidation of anyone foolish enough to oppose him. Do we really have any idea of what is best for us? Are we really in a position to declare that we know, better than God, what is good for us?

But at the theological level, a far more profound argument comes into play. It is God who created us, not we ourselves. Can we really pretend that anyone other than our creator knows what is best for us? Can we really hope to stand in the place of God and gain reliable insights into our origins, our present situation, and our future goal?

To go back to the image introduced earlier, we are on the Road and need to be able to climb to the Balcony. In order to know what is right for us, we need to know where we are going. We need dependable knowledge of what our future is meant to hold for us, in order that we can move towards achieving that goal. But what *is* the future goal of humanity? For what purpose were we created? It is here that we need to attend to God.

The true goal of humanity is to be united (perhaps we should say reunited?) with God. We have been created in the image of God with the ultimate aim of finding our rest in him. The love of God is concerned with enabling us to achieve our true and God-given potential—that is, to find peace and fulfillment with the living and loving God. Yet through sin, we have a natural tendency to desire things that are ruinous and inappropriate, perhaps without realizing that they are so.

Augustine of Hippo, perhaps one of the wisest critics of naive notions of human goodness, made this point with his famous analogy of a pair of scales. Some, he suggested, saw the human will as being like a pair of perfectly balanced scales. Right and wrong, good and evil, can thus be weighed up in the respective scale pans, and a balanced judgment reached. But, Augustine asked, what about sin? What of the corruption of human nature? The human will is actually like a pair of scales in which one of the pans is already loaded. There is a perceptible bias towards evil. It may vary from one person to another, but it is there. Left to our own devices, we will tend to choose the visible over the invisible and the creation over the creator. As a result, humans will often find it difficult to desire what is right, let alone to achieve it.

Love, in the trivial, human sense of the term, would not merely respect this situation; it would pamper it, by indulging the desires which arise from it. But this cannot be allowed to pass for the love of God. The love of God wishes to *transform* our situation, to liberate us from the tyranny of sin, and to allow us to desire and receive those things which are best for us. We must be liberated from our infatuation with things which threaten to prevent us from achieving our purpose and finding our goal.

The great prize which is set before us is none other than a relationship with God himself. But our vision is so distorted by sin that we see nothing but the lesser prizes around us. We are called by God to find our rest in him. But our hearing is so dulled that we hear only the voices of the world and its transient goals. We settle for the shadows of the grand delights for which we were created. So powerful is the hold of sin upon us that we have lowered our sights, fixing them upon the creation rather than the creator. So love, in the full and Christian sense of the term, must free us from this mess. Sin, like a swamp, bogs us down, preventing us from breaking free. So how can we be liberated?

The first step towards freedom is invariably taken only after we realize that we are imprisoned. If we are to long for liberation, we must realize that we are in bondage. Love must therefore tell us that we are lost before it can delight us with the declaration that we have been found. We, who think we know it all and know it best, must be brought to our senses. The reassuring set of beliefs that we have woven around ourselves like a cocoon must be unraveled. For instance, we do not fear death if we overlook its existence or if we believe that it happens only to others. God is obliged to bring about the funeral of this great myth—the myth of our personal immortality and the permanence of the world. These things must pass, and we shall pass with them. God will live on—and so can we, in union with him—but not if we cling steadfastly to the world and its values.

The suffering and the death of those we know and love break down the pretense of human permanence. We do not want to admit our own mortality. We find it deeply threatening to accept that the world and all those we love will one day pass beyond our grasp. It is so much more reassuring to believe that we and the world will go on forever, that we will be able to hold on to all the glittering prizes which we win during life. But suffering strips away our illusions of immortality. It causes anxiety to rear its ugly, yet revealing head. It batters down the gates of the citadel of illusions. It confronts us with the harsh facts of life and makes us ask those hard questions which have the power to erode falsehood and propel us away from the false security and transient rewards of the world toward our loving God.

"Funerals," a colleague once remarked to me, "are intended to remind those present that they are still alive—for the time being." Hospitals too are powerful symbols of human frailty and mortality, tokens of our vulnerability. Think of sin as a force, a power which opposes our coming home to God. It is like gravity, pulling things down. Our innate human inertia, made worse by sin, encourages us to remain within our comfortable view of the world, and not to inquire too deeply about its foundations. It is easier to close our eyes to the signs of loss, parting, and transience which surround us and which threaten to undermine our cozy assumptions. If eternity intersects our history at any point, it is at those moments when we realize that we, like all of humanity, are ephemeral creatures whose lot, if limited to the world of the senses, must indeed be an unhappy one.

Yet it need not be. Our eyes need to be lifted to catch a glimpse of another country and our ears alerted to hear its music. We are tied to this earth by sin, like gravity; something needs to be done to break its hold. Suffering, though tragic, is not pointless. It is the pin which bursts the balloon of our delusions, and opens the way to an urgent and passionate wrestling with the reality of death and the question of what lies beyond. It is only by breaking the surly bonds which shackle us to this dying world that we can reach out and embrace the greatest and finest prize we can ever attain—being enfolded in the love of God.

There is an irony here. Love is active in something which appears to deny love. The passionate care of God for his creatures shines through something which seems to deny that care, just as the light of the sun pierces through clouds. Perhaps the finest discussion of this point is by Martin Luther, who made the suffering of Christ and his people the centerpiece of his theology of the cross. How, Luther asked, could a loving God tolerate suffering? His answer takes the following form.

All Christian thought about the nature and purposes of God must be grounded in the cross of Christ. It is here that true theology and the knowledge of God are to be found. The cross puts everything to the test. In the words of Nicholas Ridley, who was martyred on October 16, 1555, *coticula fidei crux*, "the cross is the touchstone of faith." The love of God, Luther stresses, is revealed *through* the suffering of Christ, not *despite* that suffering. The Christian church came into being through that suffering, and shall share in that suffering before finally sharing in the glory of the risen Christ.

Luther then draws a central distinction. Sometimes God works in a way which is obviously consistent with his nature, a way of action which Luther terms *opus proprium Dei*, "the

proper work of God." But at other times, God works in a way
which initially seems to contradict his nature, yet on further
reflection is seen to be totally consistent with it. Luther refers
to this as *opus alienum Dei*, "the strange work of God." As an
example, he suggests we think about God's condemnation of
sinners. Initially, this seems to contradict what we know of
God. Is not God merciful and compassionate?

But then we realize how superficial this idea of God is. It
treats God as sickly sweet and sentimental, and ignores the
whole question of our sin and his righteousness. Knowing that
we are condemned alerts us to the reality of our situation—that
we are sinners, that we stand under the wrath of God, and that
we seem to have no claim whatsoever to mercy and forgiveness. So we turn in our hopelessness to God; we abandon our
pretensions of adequacy and learn of his mercy and grace; we
repent of our sin and receive forgiveness and mercy. Something which initially seems to contradict God's compassion
turns out to be consistent with it. God uses means which seem
to be out of line with his nature in order to bring about a goal
which is obviously true to his nature.

Think of suffering as "the strange work of God." It is not
an end in itself, but a means to a greater end—that of bringing
us home to God, where suffering is transfigured and eventually defeated. Just as Christ defeated death by his own death,
so human suffering proves to hold the key to our own eventual
transformation. The "proper work of God" is our salvation;
suffering allows God to achieve that end. Far from being an
utter absurdity, by the grace of God suffering is able to serve a
purpose.

Luther asks that we take suffering seriously and learn
why it is the cross, the symbol of suffering, which stands at the
center of our faith. Perhaps more than any other Christian
writer, he acknowledges the reality and pain of the suffering of
Christ on the cross and of believers as they share in that suffering. The Christian church is an extension of the passion of
Christ. We are called to be members of the suffering people of

God. But Luther also asks that we see beyond suffering, that we do not limit the power and presence of God to what we experience. The resurrection reminds us that, despite all appearances, God was indeed a participant at Calvary. Just as those present at the crucifixion failed to recognize God's presence at that dreadful scene, so we fail to realize that God can be present in human suffering, and can transfigure it.

FIVE

Dissatisfaction
with the World

M AN IS THE ONLY animal that laughs and weeps, for he is the only animal that is struck by the difference between what things are and what they might have been," William Hazlitt wrote. Many people are profoundly dissatisfied with this world. Deep within themselves they sense that there must be something better somewhere. These feelings are real and important, and they serve a vitally important function. Our natural instinct is to protest and shout out, "Why can't the world be better? Because it's not better, we don't want to believe in God!"

But then theology asks for a hearing. First, it points out that we are judging the reality against an ideal. Dissatisfaction with our present situation does not necessarily imply that a better alternative exists. It is like comparing our own lives with those lived by a story-book prince, or a fairy-tale princess. It might provoke a sense of wistful longing for a happier land, but there is no guarantee that such a land exists.

Why do we possess such a deep-seated sense that things could be better than this? Where does this sense come from? An important answer is provided by a distinguished group of Christian writers, from Augustine to Milton, who argued that the profound sense of dissatisfaction with many aspects of the world as we know it is to be explained as a nostalgia, a sense of longing for a lost Eden, a place where suffering and death did not exist. This memory of Eden is also an anticipation of the heavenly Jerusalem, where suffering and death will once more cease to exist as the "bliss of Eden" (Milton) is restored.

Our sense of dissatisfaction is thus a memory of this haunting "bliss of Eden." It arises from a yearning for the innocence of the first days of creation, which will one day be restored through the process of redemption in Christ. So this sense of dissatisfaction is also prophetic. It points ahead to the fulfillment of the Christian hope in the world to come. There must be a better world than this, and that will come to pass in the heavenly Jerusalem. It is at this point that the Christian hope begins to make its presence felt, for the gospel declares that one day such a world will exist. It insists that the world we now know will be replaced by a new heaven and a new earth. Thus this sense of dissatisfaction is God-given, intended to remind us that this world is not our home. It is intended to make us yearn for the world which is to come.

Naturally, this will not satisfy the armchair critics of God, who will promptly declare that they could have created a universe devoid of any suffering and pain. But could they really? Sadly (for we would like to believe them), this invariably turns out to be the rhetoric of dissatisfaction, which promises a better world as a matter of principle, rather than of fact. The idea of a pain-free world is just about as utopian a delusion as you can find anywhere. A world without suffering would be a world without life as we know it. Suffering is the price we pay for living. And though that price tag is expensive, it is something that most are willing to pay. We shall return to this theme in a later chapter.

Secondly, theology reminds us that this is a fallen world—a world which has been ruined by sin. It assures us that our feelings of dissatisfaction are genuine and important because they give birth to the hope of a new earth and a new heaven, in which suffering and pain will be a thing of the past.

Theology makes sense of this feeling of longing for an ideal world in which there is no suffering. Suffering is like a gadfly, continually irritating us, provoking us to ask hard questions. How can the suffering of this world be alleviated? When will this world become a better place? And it is not just Christians who have wrestled with these questions.

One of the most important—and until recently, one of the most influential—secular answers to this question was provided by Karl Marx. The Marxist analysis of human experience recognizes this feeling of dissatisfaction with the way the world is, and claims the ability to cure it. After the revolution, this sense of dissatisfaction (which is a direct result of capitalism) will disappear. But in those parts of the world where the revolution came, the sense of dissatisfaction obstinately remained. The revolution failed to get rid of suffering. Pain, and all the questions which its presence raises, remained unanswered and unresolved. Marxism, like other secular answers to the riddle of suffering, failed to satisfy.

The New Testament also promises the ending of suffering. The sufferings of the present age can only be ended through the final coming of the kingdom of God (Rom. 8:18–25). The present sufferings are like birth-pangs. They anticipate the coming of new life. This coming kingdom will one day happen to every believer, through the death and resurrection of the body, and joyful entry into eternal life in the New Jerusalem. It is this hope which keeps Christian believers going in life. Indeed, it is our anticipation of the life of the New Jerusalem, in which suffering is ended and tears are wiped away, that makes us so dissatisfied with the world as we now know it.

One of the finest expressions of this feeling may be found in the famous words of Augustine of Hippo: "You have made us for yourself, and our hearts are restless until they rest in you." Throughout Augustine's reflections, especially in the *Confessions*, the same theme recurs. We are doomed to remain incomplete in our present existence.

There is a sense of postponement, of longing, of wistful yearning, of groaning under the strain of having to tolerate the sufferings of the present, when the future offers so much. Perhaps the finest statement of this exquisite agony is found in Paul's epistle to the Romans: "We know that the whole creation has been groaning as in the pains of childbirth right up to the present time. Not only so, but we ourselves, who have the first-fruits of the Spirit, groan inwardly as we wait eagerly for ... the redemption of our bodies" (Rom 8:22–23).

Theology, then, acknowledges the reality of our distress at the presence of suffering in the world. But it has things to say that we need to hear. Christians feel the pain of suffering so intensely because of the vision of the creation as it will be on that day when suffering ends and human tears are wiped dry for the last time. Why can it not happen sooner? Why does God not end the present order now? Why wait?

It is on precisely this note that the Revelation of St. John ends. Having glimpsed the joy of the New Jerusalem and tasted the peace of the new heaven and the new earth, John cannot bear to wait any longer. "Come, Lord Jesus," he cries (Rev. 22:20). And we share his feelings, as we survey the sadness and sorrow of the world.

Much the same feelings are expressed in Paul's letter to the Christians at Philippi, in which the apostle finds himself torn between the joy of going to be with Christ, and the work that remains for him on earth. "For to me, to live is Christ and to die is gain ... I am torn between the two: I desire to depart and be with Christ, which is better by far; but it is more necessary for you that I remain in the body" (Phil. 1:21–24).

Suffering makes us yearn to be with Christ in the heavenly realms. It strengthens and nourishes our hope and thus makes us impatient with the way things are, of which suffering is a symptom. But as the example of Jesus Christ reminds us, resurrection lies on the far side of suffering. That hope is enough to keep us going in the face of suffering and to make us want to share that hope with others who suffer without faith.

SIX

Suffering and the
God of the Philosophers

SINCE HISTORY BEGAN, the existence of pain, suffering, and evil
in the world has been recognized as a problem. Yet Christian
theology has learned to live with this reality. It is not as if suffering were a well-kept secret, the existence of which has suddenly been sprung upon a world which fervently believed it
did not exist.

Yet some would have us believe that suffering is something new. It is true that the last hundred years have seen new
horrors of suffering, through wars of unparalleled destructive-
ness and viciousness, through the deliberate causation of
famine, and through the ruthless exploitation of the environment and of ethnic minorities. For reasons such as this, we are
told that God cannot be taken seriously anymore.

But why should we accept this reckless assertion? Human
sinfulness has caused untold human suffering. The great liberal
vision of moral progress through the harnessing of technology
and the sciences has collapsed. The technology which was
meant to alleviate suffering has been used to cause pain and
death. The sciences have been remorselessly exploited to
develop new and more efficient ways to eliminate unwanted
human beings. It is not the idea of God, but a doctrinaire belief
in the goodness of human nature, which has been shattered by

the sufferings of the present age. And if that is a hard lesson to learn, it nevertheless needs to be learned.

Christian writers before the seventeenth century did not believe that suffering posed any serious threat to Christian belief. Indeed, I spent many years working through most of the major works on Christian theology written between the twelfth and sixteenth centuries, and I cannot recall any of them treating the reality of suffering as a serious obstacle to Christian faith.

But now the situation has changed. Why is suffering seen as a challenge to faith, as never before? The answer lies in a dramatic development which took place during the seventeenth century, and which, according to many scholars, lies at the roots of modern atheism. Anxious to make Christianity intellectually respectable, a number of writers—such as Leonard Lessius and Marin Mersenne—argued that the best defense of the gospel was provided by philosophy. To defend the Christian faith it was advisable to set aside traditional ways of justifying it and to rely instead upon the wisdom of philosophy.

So instead of concentrating upon the significance of Jesus Christ for the question of whether God exists and what he is like, an appeal was made directly and exclusively to reason. Instead of an appeal to the Christian experience of the Holy Spirit, an appeal was made to nature. Reason and nature were thus the testing grounds on which the credibility of Christianity was judged. The end result was inevitable. Under the influence of these well-meaning but misguided people, Christianity entered into the defense of the existence of God without being able to appeal to anything recognizably or distinctly Christian. The resources that had served the gospel for century after century were discarded as relics of a past era.

Things went from bad to worse through the impact of the seventeenth-century philosopher René Descartes, who thought he had invented a neat and watertight defense of his faith. Arguing that God was a totally perfect being, Descartes developed a number of interesting philosophical arguments for the existence of God on the basis of this assumption. But the enormous emphasis which came to be placed upon the perfection of God was totally compromised by the undeniable fact of the existence of evil and suffering. How could a perfect being allow such imperfection to exist? Descartes's "god" is not the God of Christianity; it is simply a philosophical idea. His defense of Christianity is actually just a defense of an idea about God that he happened to develop.

Blaise Pascal may be numbered among the greatest French philosophers, scientists, and mathematicians, but he was also profoundly aware of the limitations of philosophical ways of thinking about God. The God of the Bible was intensely personal; Pascal believed passionately that philosophy had thrown away this insight. After his death, Pascal's colleagues found a crumpled piece of paper sewed up inside his shirt. It was obviously so important to him that he wanted to carry it with him everywhere he went, pressed close to his heart. The words on this piece of paper have become legendary and are intensely relevant to our theme: "God of Abraham, God of Isaac, God of Jacob, not of philosophers and scholars, God of Jesus Christ, my God and your God. Your God shall be my God." Here is a perceptive personal declaration of faith, and an emphatic rejection of mere ideas of God in favor of the personal reality of God in people's lives.

Now there is nothing wrong with philosophy. Philosophy makes us ask hard questions about how we know anything. It forces us to think about our words and ideas, and to make sure we know what we are doing when we use them. The problems develop when some philosophers argue that human reason itself can tell us exactly what God is like. This overlooks the fact that God has already taken the trouble to tell us what he is like.

The god of the philosophers is basically little more than a perfect, ideal, and abstract being, constructed out of the distilled elements of human benevolence. The characteristics of this god are primarily omnipotence, omniscience, and goodness. The credibility of this god is instantly compromised by suffering. As Alasdair MacIntyre, one of the most perceptive of modern philosophers, remarks, "The God in whom the nineteenth and twentieth centuries came to disbelieve had been invented only in the seventeenth century." The god of philosophical theology is a human invention, a product of human reason. Yet the God to whom Christian faith and theology respond is a living and loving being, who makes himself known to us through Christ, Scripture, and personal experience—including, as we shall see, suffering.

As Pascal so clearly saw, the philosophical idea of God bears little relation to the God of Jesus Christ—*our* God. Somehow, the philosophical idea of God seems bleak and dreary, both in itself and in comparison with the joyful Christian experience of God. It reminds me of Jonathan Edwards's celebrated remarks to Samuel Johnson: "You are a philosopher, Dr. Johnson. I have tried too in my time to be a philosopher, but I don't know how. Cheerfulness was always breaking in." The theologian, steeped in the knowledge of the resurrection of the suffering and crucified Christ, brings a certain sense of joy to the question of suffering—a joy which is conspicuously absent from the philosophical discussion of the question.

And what of the moral side of things? Descartes's god, like Aristotle's Unmoved Mover, stands callously to one side uninvolved and detached while the world suffers. Like a Victorian lord of the manor enjoying a sumptuous lifestyle while remaining indifferent to the deprivation and poverty of the lower classes, the god of Descartes is an offense and a scandal. Small wonder that there was a clamor for its abolition.

But the God and Father of our Lord Jesus Christ is very different. Here is no Unmoved Mover. Here is the creator of the world, who chose to enter into the pain, sorrow, and sadness of the fallen world in order to restore it to its wholeness. Here is a God who knows pain at first hand, who shares the woes of his people. No longer can we speak about suffering alone and unnoticed. The experience of suffering has been taken up into the life of God.

There is much more that could be said on this point, and we shall reflect further upon it presently. But the main argument is clear: the God of Christianity and the god of Descartes are different. The death of the latter (which, as we stressed, is a relatively recent invention) need be the cause of little mourning. Christians now need to ensure that the world learns of the divine care and compassion made known through the passion and death of Jesus Christ.

SEVEN

The Price of Life

I ARRANGED TO MEET an Oxford colleague, whom I had not seen for some time, for lunch one day. We talked about our lives, swapped news, and discussed our mutual friends—the sort of things any friends do when they get together after a period of absence. My friend then told me a story about a young woman who had been seriously injured in a traffic accident. Although she survived the accident, she would have to endure a degree of pain for the remainder of her life.

My friend was in a reflective mood. I remember his saying something like, "She was so badly hurt, that she is probably going to be in some pain for the rest of her days. You know, if she had been an animal—a horse or a dog—she would have been put to sleep." That remark stayed in my mind, even though (I have to confess) I have forgotten just about everything else we talked about that day.

Suffering is the price we pay for being alive. More than that; it is the price we pay for being human. We are willing to terminate the life of an animal to prevent suffering, but human life is different. Human existence seems to be something priceless. Suffering does not make life meaningless or valueless. Suffering is not an add-on feature which we can dispense with, but a vital aspect of our existence as humans. To live without suffering would be to live in a pretend world, under permanent sedation not only from its trials and tribulations, but also from its joys and pleasures.

But there is more to it than this. Suffering brings us to maturity. We learn through suffering. There is much truth in the old Greek saying, *pathemata mathemata* "suffering is education." Suffering makes us more sensitive and compassionate people, more aware of the needs and anxieties of others. It brings out the full power of human creativity. It is no accident that some of the best art seems to arise from situations of pain or hardship. Van Gogh's paintings echo his personal sadness. Some of Beethoven's greatest music dates from the period of his life when he was devastated by the thought of becoming deaf and thus being cut off from the musical world of his own making.

Suffering often brings out the full potential of human beings, unleashing a creativity which is too easily stifled by smugness and security. Orson Welles is merely one of many writers to note that material well-being and affluence seem to suppress the power of the human imagination. Renaissance Italy, with all its struggles and suffering, produced some of the finest works of art humanity has ever known. But what, Welles asked, has pampered, neutral, and prosperous Switzerland ever contributed to the history of human culture? The cuckoo clock.

To be human is to want to be free. Freedom matters to people. Think of how many wars have been fought in order to preserve, or restore, the freedom of nations. Think of the great civil rights protests, which demanded freedom for the citizens of these nations. The yearning for liberty seems to be a basic feature, not merely of human civilization, but of human nature itself.

I remember once hearing an interview with a prominent politician in a small eastern European nation that was demanding freedom from its much larger neighbor, then known as the Soviet Union. The interviewer pressed him on a significant point. What about the economic consequences? Wouldn't it spell economic ruin to break away from its larger neighbor? "Maybe—but we want to be free to make our own mistakes!" was the indignant reply.

Children leave their parental home, setting to one side its familiarity and security. Why? Partly because they want to break free from it. However much they may value their parents, they want to live their own lives, to make their own decisions, and to learn from their own mistakes. Deep down, all of us know of our need to learn things for ourselves. We don't want to accept everything on authority. That seems too much like a lapse into blind and mindless dictatorship. We want to check things out for ourselves. And that means having the freedom to do so.

But what is the price of this freedom? Freedom implies that we are free to make mistakes, to do things which hurt others, to cause evil. Jean-Paul Sartre, easily among the most perceptive of the existentialist writers, spoke of humans as being "condemned to freedom." In other words, we have no choice but to be free and to live with the consequences of that freedom. If we were simply a form of machine or computer, programmed to do only things that we found acceptable, there would be no problem about evil. We wouldn't do wrong things. We wouldn't be allowed to do them. We wouldn't cause suffering or evil. But then we wouldn't be free, either.

So we have two options: to be free in a restricted sense of the word (only to do good), or to be free in a fuller sense of the word (including the worrying possibility of being free to make mistakes, and do evil). The first is fraught with the risk of paternalism: "Don't do this. It wouldn't be good for you." The original sin of Genesis chapter 3 is based on a rejection of precisely this sort of freedom. The first man and woman were free to do exactly what they pleased, providing they did not do something which they were told was forbidden.

But they did it. They didn't want to be told what was off limits and what wasn't. They wanted to be like God, free to decide what was right and what was wrong. They wanted to set their own limits and live within them. The Christian tradition has seen in this demand for autonomy the root of all suffering. It seems that a central element of fallen human nature is a rugged sense of independence: we do not like being told what we may and may not do.

So we have freedom—a freedom to do evil, a freedom to avoid and disobey God. God leaves us room to be human. He makes space for us to make mistakes. God pulls himself back from his creation in order to allow it to exercise the freedom which he chose to allow it. (It is pointless to speak of God endowing his creatures with freedom, only to refuse to allow them to exercise that freedom.) Yet in the exercise of that freedom, we may see the origins of much of the tragic suffering of the world.

But would we rather be without that freedom? Paradoxically, it is something that we can never abandon, even though we find it difficult to live with its results. As Sartre rightly saw, to be human is to be free to commit evil and to inflict suffering. Part of our problem with suffering is that we are reluctant to allow that there is something wrong with human nature which allows us to abuse our God-given freedom. Yet the casualty of this observation is not God; it is humans who persist in their deluded and naive belief about the goodness of human nature.

There is another aspect of suffering which we need to note here. That is the sheer tragedy of the human predicament. In everyday use, the word *tragedy* tends to mean something like disastrous, pitiful, or pathetic. But here it means more than that. It points to our powerlessness to change things. It hints at our lack of control over our own destiny. It declares our inability to change things and our sense of anger, mingled with despair, at the way things are. Part of the offense of suffering lies in the fact that we cannot control it. Suffering is part of the chaos and disorder of sin. We have been able to master the skills of putting people on the moon and discovering the hidden secrets of the most distant planets, yet we cannot put an end to human suffering on earth. One of the reasons why modern human beings find suffering so offensive is that its existence points to the limits of human achievement. Despite all human advances in civilization, suffering remains unmastered and untamed.

Many cultures have developed ways of coping with the tragic side of life. They know that nature is difficult to control and to predict. Suffering takes its place among the changes and chances of life. Suffering does not seem to have been a major philosophical problem in the Middle Ages, nor is it today for countless millions in Africa and Latin America. But in the highly developed societies of the West, suffering is a problem, perhaps because these societies have long lost sight of cultural resources for coping with suffering. It is not so much a theological, as a cultural, issue. So how has this problem arisen?

In the West, and especially in the United States, a form of "cultural Pelagianism" has gained the upper hand. Pelagianism was a movement, based in Rome in the early fifth century, which asserted that human beings were in total control of their situation, including their relationship to God. This overconfident worldview overlooked the tragic side of human nature with its obvious weaknesses and failings. Pelagianism was, at heart, a delusion, but a delusion which many people passionately wanted to believe in. They didn't want to face up to the hard facts of life, which suggested that human beings were not in control of things and needed the grace of God if they were to survive and prosper.

Just as Pelagius declared that human beings had total control over themselves and their destinies, so modern Western society wants to believe that it can control every aspect of life. Yet although it is enormously technologically advanced, Western society has discovered that it cannot defeat death any more than it can control suffering.

Suffering thus causes offense by pricking this bubble of optimism. It is a painful reminder of the limitations of human nature and human culture. Suffering hurts because it points to definite and disconcerting limits to human abilities. At least some of the theological fuss about suffering reflects this sense of outrage and offense. This explains the paradox that Westerners, who are among the most privileged of the human race, who enjoy standards of living which are astonishing by other standards, and who, through excellent medical services, suffer less than anyone else make suffering into a bigger theological problem than it need be.

So how should Christians respond to this? Partly, by asking that we recover our awareness of our limitations as human beings. Suffering is threatening because it is a reminder of our powerlessness to control our world. We need to accept those limitations and realize that, on account of them, suffering will be an inevitable part of human existence. It is the price we pay for being human.

EIGHT

What Was God Doing on the Cross?

T HE CROSS. Those two words sum up the greatest story that the world has ever been told. It is hard to read that story without being deeply moved. The majestic and dignified suffering of Jesus often causes people to ask deep questions. Why did this wonderful person have to suffer in this way? What was *God* doing on the cross?

The first answer to that question might, at first sight, seem a little trivial. *He was there.* Three men were crucified at Calvary. But there was something very different about the man on the central cross. He was content to be "numbered with the transgressors" (Isa. 53:12), but he was not among their number. The meaning of the cross can only be grasped if we realize the identity of Jesus. As the resurrection made clear (Rom. 1:3–4), it was the Son of God who died on that cross, in order that we might live (John 3:16).

Christian theology uses the word *incarnation* when it talks about Jesus becoming a human being. To talk about the incarnation, or about "God incarnate," is to declare that God became one of us in Jesus Christ. If Jesus is God, then the sight of Jesus on the cross offers us many amazing insights about God, each of them worthy of a book in itself.

For example, if Jesus is God, then he is the best visual aid for God that the world has ever known. We all know how difficult it can be to speak about God at times, partly because we find it hard to picture him. Very often *God* is little more than an abstract idea. Now, God has authorized us to think of Jesus when we try to think about him. To have seen Jesus is to have seen the Father (John 14:9). Jesus is a window into God.

Try to imagine that you are talking to someone about the character of God. You want to explain how awesome God's love is. Without Jesus, you might find yourself faltering a little, as you grasp for words to try to explain the wonder of that love. You might wander from one cliché to another: "It's just too wonderful for words"; "It is beyond human telling."

Now see how the incarnation changes all this. No longer are you at a loss for words. You can ask your friend to imagine Jesus trudging his lonely and painful way to the cross, there to die in shame and agony—not for anything he did, but for our sake. Imagine the love which this action shows. *This* is what the love of God is like!

From the perspective of the Road, Jesus Christ may seem like a fellow-traveler, someone who shares our journey along that difficult and winding way we call the life of faith. But from the Balcony, he is seen to be very different from all of us. Here is God—the same God who made the heaven and earth—who has chosen to spend time on the Road. He didn't have to; he wanted to. And his presence on that Road changes everything. Not only can we journey knowing that we are in the best of company; but we also have new confidence in the reliability of that Road, and are reassured of the certainty of reaching its final destination.

The second thing which God was doing on the cross was *showing us how much he loves us*. Once we have realized that it is none other than the Son of God who is dying on the cross, a whole new world opens up to us. People thought that God had abandoned Christ, but in reality he was there, working out the salvation of the world. The crowds around the cross called on

Jesus to save himself, but he stayed there to the bitter end and saved us instead. He bore his suffering on account of his love for us. The Son of God willingly died for people like you and me.

Now we might be able to understand someone giving his life for especially good people. But the amazing thing is this: While we were still sinners, Christ died for us (Rom. 5:8). As Paul puts it, "I live by faith in the Son of God, who loved me and gave himself for me."

The greatest demonstration of love that human beings can manage is usually their last, as well as their greatest. They give the most precious thing they possess, the gift of life itself. "Greater love has no one than this, that one lay down his life for his friends" (John 15:13).

A medical orderly caught up in the brutality of the First World War was crouching in the security of his trench somewhere in Flanders when he saw one of his comrades fall wounded some distance from the safety of his own lines. Rather than leave him to die, the medical orderly crawled the considerable distance to where the man lay, and with great difficulty dragged him back. As the orderly lowered his friend into the trench, he himself was hit by a sniper's bullet and mortally wounded. As he lay dying, he was told that his friend would live, and he was able to die with that knowledge. He had given his life for a friend.

Doubtless many other examples of this sort of behavior in battle could be given. It illustrates human love forced to its absolute limits. The man who gives his life for his friend does not even enjoy the satisfaction of his future company. All is given and nothing received—except, perhaps, a brief satisfaction that something worthwhile has been achieved.

In the death of Jesus Christ on the cross, we can see the amazing love of God revealed to a wondering world. Christ is God in human flesh; in the image of the dying Christ, we see God himself, giving himself up for his people. Charles Wesley exults in this thought:

> Amazing love! how can it be
> That thou, my God shouldst die for me?

And:

> 'Tis mystery all! th' immortal dies!
> Who can explore his strange design?
> In vain the first-born seraph tries
> To sound the depths of love divine!

Here is no surrogate, no representative, no delegation. Here is God himself, willingly giving himself for us, in order that we might have life in all its fullness.

But there is more to the cross than this. Part of God's love is his firm purpose and power to change us, to get us out of the mess we are in on account of sin. A third vital aspect of what God was doing on the cross, then, can be summed up like this: *God was breaking the stranglehold of sin in our lives.* The life, suffering, and death of the Son of God delivers us from the penalty of sin, begins to break the power of sin, and will one day finally deliver us from the presence of sin. Through the cross of Christ, God set in motion a chain of events. Some of those events have already happened; some are in the process of happening; some have yet to happen in all their fullness. We will speak further of this in a later chapter.

What was God doing on the cross? In the fourth place, *he was liberating us from the fear of death.* So much of Western culture is terrorized by the fear of death. People find it difficult even to talk about death because it is so threatening a subject. Yet through his cross and resurrection, Jesus liberates his people from the fear. Jesus shares our human nature, so that "by his death he might destroy him who holds the power of death—that is the devil—and free those who all their lives were held in slavery by their fear of death" (Heb. 2:14–15). Through Christ's death and resurrection, God has gained a great and famous victory over death. And that victory can be ours! Listen to Paul, as he concludes the great exposition of the reality and relevance of his resurrection in 1 Corinthians 15:

What Was God Doing on the Cross?

"Thanks be to God! He gives us the victory through our Lord Jesus Christ" (v. 57).

Now there is much more that can be said about the cross than this. A textbook would be required to do justice to the many themes of the gospel which converge on the cross of Christ. The theme of the reality of forgiveness would be of major importance, as would that of the costliness of forgiveness. So too would the theme of the need for people to respond to the cross, to allow it to have an impact upon our fallen and broken lives. But this book is about suffering, and we must therefore ask ourselves how the cross relates to this theme.

The fifth, and perhaps the most important answer to this question for our purposes relates to *the presence and participation of God in suffering*. As we have seen, God was present at Calvary. He came down from the Balcony to the Road and walked among us, suffering and wondering, like us. He knows at first hand what it is like to suffer. Faith provides us with this vital insight. Theology insists that we value and relish it.

So the Creator enters into his creation, not as a curious tourist, but as a committed savior. He does not observe it from the Balcony, but comes down to the level of the Road, to be with us. This astonishing act of self-emptying and humility is celebrated in the Christian festival of Christmas, when we recall the One who, though rich beyond all splendor, became poor for our sake. As the Nicene Creed puts it, "for us, and for our salvation, he came down from heaven."

We might think of some more lines from Charles Wesley's hymn, "And Can It Be?"

> He left his father's throne above,
> So free, so infinite his grace.
> Emptied himself of all but love,
> And bled for Adam's helpless race.

The love of God expressed in the suffering of Christ thus declares firmly that suffering has, by the grace of God, its place within his redemptive purposes. The early church was passionately concerned to safeguard insights such as these. One particular threat was posed by the heresy known as *docetism,* which taught that Jesus was not really human at all. He just seemed to suffer; he just seemed to be in pain. (The word *docetism* comes form the Greek verb *dokein* "to seem.") Rightly, the theologians of the early church saw that it was vital to defend the reality of the suffering and death of Christ. If they were not real, then he did not really confront the forces of evil which threaten us. He did not really experience the pain and suffering that we experience.

Now some will point out, rightly, that God knows everything. He did not need to *experience* suffering to know what it is like. But we can turn that observation on its head. For it reminds us, first of all, that God *chose* to suffer. God "accommodates himself to our weakness" (John Calvin). He knows that we find it difficult to accept that he, too, knows about suffering. So, for our benefit, he makes it as clear as possible.

And secondly, there is a real difference between knowing *about* something and knowing it firsthand. I can know about suffering by watching my friends who are in pain. But I am an observer, not a participant. I am on the Balcony, rather than the Road. As a young man, I remember people telling me how dreadfully painful migraine headaches were. Yet although I knew that these headaches were painful, this was a second-hand insight. After my first experience of a migraine headache, however, I felt a new sympathy for those who suffer from them. I knew firsthand what they had been through. We would call the first kind of knowledge *cognitive,* and the second *experiential.* The crucifixion of Christ is a public demonstration that God knows suffering firsthand.

I once got into conversation with a student who was in a state of depression. He found his situation difficult to cope with, for it seemed that there was little that could be done about it. At his bedside he had a self-help book written by someone who had himself been through a period of depression and had subsequently put his experiences on paper. Every now and then this student would read some passages from that book. He would feel much better for having done so. "That's just how I feel!" he would exclaim. "That person really understands me!" Such thoughts helped him cope with his depression because he felt that someone else had made it through what he was currently experiencing. There was light at the end of the tunnel.

The passion stories of the gospels are like that self-help book. They bring the insights of the Balcony to those of us on the Road. They tell of someone who really understands suffering, and who has been through it himself. "Jesus Christ must know how I feel when I suffer. This is a real figure of flesh and blood who went through the same sorts of things that I experience. And if Jesus Christ is really God, then God must have experienced all this pain and misery firsthand himself. I can relate to this God."

Such thoughts bring us to one of the most moving features of the gospel. The God whom we know through Jesus Christ is compassionate and sympathetic. He understands us.

NINE

The Compassion
of Our God

W<small>E TEND TO READ</small> Scripture too quickly. Certainly, there are some passages that need to be gulped down like a refreshing and cooling drink on a hot day. But there are others that need to be sipped and savored slowly as if they were a classic vintage. One such passage is that which opens one of Paul's most reflective letters, the second letter to the Corinthians, in which the themes of human suffering and divine consolation compete for attention:

> Praise be to the God and Father of our Lord Jesus Christ, the Father of compassion and the God of all comfort, who comforts us in all our troubles, so that we can comfort those in any trouble with the comfort we ourselves have received from God. For just as the sufferings of Christ flow over into our lives, so also through Christ our comfort overflows (2 Cor. 1:3–5).

God is "the Father of compassion." The word *compassion* comes from the Latin and has the basic meaning of "suffering alongside someone." It possesses extended meanings such as "kindness," "consideration," or "clemency." To be compassionate is to be able to set yourself alongside one who is suffering, to share his pain and anguish. The word *sympathetic* has much the same meaning, but derives from the Greek. Christ is our sympathetic high priest (Heb. 4:15). He has been through all that we are being asked to go through. Knowing that, we may approach him with confidence, because he understands our plight. Indeed, he has shared it, and thus he has created a powerful bond of sympathy between himself and ourselves.

This thought provides us with more than spiritual insight and consolation. It also gives us a real stimulus to alleviate suffering because the suffering of the world grieves God. The pages of history are stained with the tears of God. By working to relieve suffering in the world, we are lessening the sadness of God, who shares in that suffering. Our suffering is his suffering; his suffering is our suffering. Perhaps the face of the crucified Christ, shot through with pain and tears, allows us to envisage how God must feel over the way his creation is groaning in pain as it awaits its liberation from bondage to decay (Rom. 8:20–21).

This thought gives us a powerful motive to work for the relief of pain and suffering in the world. Many Christians find the overt secularism of many relief agencies disconcerting, and for this reason they are less committed to caring for the needs of others than they might otherwise be. But theology has an insight which must be heard here. By seeking to alleviate the hardships suffered by others in this harsh world, we are working to ease the pain of God at the suffering of his creation. God suffers along with his people. By lessening their sadness and suffering, we are bringing a smile to the face of God. It does not really matter whether this takes the form of caring for the needs of the old and infirm, giving money to avert global famines and floods, or spending time talking with those who are sad and lonely. By doing any of these, we are meeting a real human need, we are fulfilling the command to love as we have been loved, and we are gladdening the father-heart of a God who chooses to suffer along with those whom he created and loves.

And in his love for us, God consoles us in our suffering. I often find my mind going back to one of the great prophetic passages of the Old Testament, which converges upon and is fulfilled by the death of Jesus Christ—the prophecy of the Suffering Servant of God in Isaiah 52 and 53. It is impossible to read this passage without being reminded of the last hours of the life of Christ. Suffering, shame, and pain cast their shadow over the entire section.

The passage appears to open with the theme of exaltation:

> See, my servant will act wisely;
> he will be raised and lifted up and highly exalted
>   (52:13).

This might immediately suggest that the servant of God will find fame, fortune, and favor in life. But soon the darker side of the theme becomes clear. Christ is indeed exalted and lifted up—he is lifted up on the cross at Calvary, for all to see and despise, in the most public and painful form of execution.

The themes of rejection, being reviled, and undergoing suffering soon come to the fore:

> He was despised and rejected by men,
> a man of sorrows, and familiar with suffering (53:3).

The suffering servant shares our human situation, drinking deeply of the bitter waters of pain and affliction. The poignancy of the passage is unmistakable. It sketches, briefly and yet with great effect, the image of a tender young life destroyed through suffering. Perhaps the thought of the utter pointlessness of it all passes through our minds.

Almost anticipating such a development, the passage moves on to reflect on the purpose of this innocent suffering:

> Surely he took up our infirmities
> and carried our sorrows,
> yet we considered him stricken by God,
> smitten by him, and afflicted.
> But he was pierced for our transgressions,
> he was crushed for our iniquities;
> the punishment that brought us peace was upon him,
> and by his wounds we are healed (53:4–5).

The first statement is astonishing, and pulls us up short. The servant is suffering, not on behalf of himself, but for us. But how? And why? The servant has the sorrow of a sinful world laid upon his shoulders, in much the same way as the priest laid the sins of his people upon the scapegoat, before driving it into the wilderness.

In some way, the servant has taken upon himself the burden of our grief and sorrow. Those looking on rush to the wrong conclusion: he has been condemned by God! But subsequent events make it clear that this is not the case. In some way, it is we who have been condemned and the suffering servant who bears our punishment. Suffering has been taken away from us and laid upon him. Through the mystery of God's compassion and care, the servant is prepared to suffer in order that others might be thought of as being righteous (53:11). He was content to be treated as if he were a sinner, bearing their sin, and suffering beside them (53:12).

This passage, perhaps more powerfully than any other, brings out the idea of the compassion of Christ. He is prepared to suffer alongside sinners, being reckoned among their number. Remember that Jesus died between two criminals—men who were sinners in the eyes of the world. What more dramatic symbol could one want of the compassion of Christ? Or what more convincing fulfillment of Christ's declaration that "It is written: 'And he was numbered with the transgressors'; and I tell you that this must be fulfilled in me" (Luke 22:37). Christ was—and was meant to be—present with those who suffered and finally died.

This is compassion in the full sense of the word. Here we see Jesus being prepared to suffer with sinners, being counted as if he were among their number, and condemned to share their fate. And he accepted this identification, making no attempt to evade its consequences. He identified with us right up to the end, joining us in this solidarity of suffering.

God has borne our sorrows on the bitter cross of Calvary. He became acquainted with our grief. This is no vague mumbling about God being "aware" of our sufferings; rather it is a glorious affirmation that God has *shared* our sufferings. God is a fellow-sufferer who understands, not someone who uncomprehendingly views our situation from a safe distance.

We need to distinguish between the related (but different) ideas of *sympathy* and *empathy*. Sympathy is the situation of having been through the same experience as someone else. You have, so to speak, suffered with them. Empathy, however, is the ability to imagine oneself in the same situation. In professional counseling empathy is of paramount importance. In order to be of use to someone who needs comforting, you try to think yourself into their situation, and ask: "How must they be feeling if they have been through this experience?" For example, suppose the person you are trying to help is dying from cancer. You, however, are perfectly fit. You try to work out what it must feel like to be dying of cancer, and thus to say and do things which might be of some use.

But try to place yourself in the place of the person who is in real need. For example, suppose that your mother has recently died and that you find yourself distressed as a result. You want to talk to someone about it. Which would you expect to find more approachable and helpful: someone whose mother is still alive, but who is prepared to think themselves into your situation, and imagine how you must feel? Or someone whose mother died not that long ago, and who instinctively knows just how you feel about it? It is basic to human nature to prefer to talk to someone who shares your suffering, someone who sympathizes. And that simple observation has important theological consequences.

Christ does not empathize with our sufferings, trying to work out how we must feel about the sorrows and woes of human existence. He already knows. He has been through them himself. He has experienced them at first hand. In short, he sympathizes with us. And that brings a new depth and quality to our prayer to Christ in such situations. As we noted earlier, we can pray to him with confidence, knowing that he already knows our needs, and has experienced them before us. Are we troubled by temptation? Christ has been through a more severe time of testing than anything we are ever likely to experience. Christ "has been tempted in every way, just as we are—yet was without sin" (Heb. 4:15). Are we troubled by suffering and pain? Remember that Christ suffered the agony of crucifixion. He knows what it is like.

There is a splendid story once told about shepherds in East Anglia, formerly the center of England's wool trade. When a shepherd died (so the story goes) he would be buried in a coffin stuffed full of wool. Now the real reason for this was probably to provide a market for wool in a time of economic depression during the Middle Ages, but people found this rather practical explanation a little unexciting and unimaginative. Another explanation was soon found for the practice: When the day of judgment came, Christ would notice the wool in the coffin and realize that this man had been a shepherd. Since he himself had once been a shepherd, he would know the pressures the man had faced—the amount of time needed to look after wayward sheep, and so on. So he would understand why he hadn't been to church much!

This story makes an important point, which we must treasure as one of the greatest of the gospel insights: Christ knows our situation as one who is compassionate. Suffering is second nature to him. And we can thus draw comfort and encouragement from him as we face the same situation in our own lives. The God of all compassion is with us, even in the valley of the shadow of death.

But how can that shadow be lifted? Let us turn to explore the theme of victory over suffering.

TEN

Christ's Victory
over Suffering

"THANKS BE TO GOD! He gives us the victory through our Lord Jesus Christ" (1 Cor. 15:57). In what sense can the cross and resurrection of Christ be seen as a *victory* over suffering? Exploring this question can help us see the problem of suffering in a totally new light.

The power of suffering lies partly in its presence, and partly in the terror that it instills. Suffering frightens us for all sorts of reasons. It is a painful experience in its own right, yet it also seems to imply other, perhaps more frightening things. An episode from my early childhood will illustrate my point.

One morning I woke up early to hear a strange noise in my bedroom. It sounded like someone knocking at my window. It was still dark, and I was terrified. That sound, a mixture of knocking and scratching, made me bury myself deep under the covers in the hope that whoever it was would go away and leave me alone. But the noise continued. Eventually morning came, and I plucked up enough courage to peek out of the covers to see what was going on.

It was a branch of a tree, snapped off by the wind during the night which was scratching, scraping, and tapping against the window. I felt like a fool for being so frightened, yet my reaction was understandable. It was not the noise itself, but the fear of the unknown, the dreadful anxiety that the noise might be caused by something sinister, that had prompted me to dive under the covers.

Suffering is like that. As a physical experience, it is vastly more painful and difficult to bear than a mere noise. But it is what suffering might imply that frightens many people. Suffering could imply meaninglessness. It could imply sin and separation from God, as Job's comforters knew only too well. It could imply that God is powerless to do anything about his world, or that he does not care for his creatures. These are some of the frightening implications of suffering. Suffering thus possesses a double cutting edge: the sheer pain and distress of the experience is driven to an unbearable intensity by what that suffering might imply.

Christ's death and resurrection draw the sting out of suffering. They declare that suffering is not meaningless. God worked out the salvation of the world through the suffering of Christ. Suffering does not always result from sin or lead to separation from God; the suffering of the sinless Christ and his resurrection to glory make this point more powerfully than we could ever have hoped. Through faith we are bonded to Christ in a "fellowship of sharing in his sufferings" (Phil. 3:10). And suffering does not mean that this world lies beyond the power or love of God. The almighty God stooped down in humility to suffer for us, to show us the full extent of his love for us. And so, just as the dawn allowed me to stop worrying about the noise at my window, the dawn of the world's new day through the resurrection of Christ stills our anxieties about the sinister implications of suffering. It remains a painful and powerful presence in our world, but its sting has been drawn. It is seen in a new light. The element of the unknown, the sinister, has been removed. We are reassured that suffering does not possess the power we once thought. The bluff of suffering has been called. Its power, though not its presence, has been defeated.

Suffering is defeated, not in the sense of being abolished, but in the sense of being turned around. Suffering, along with its ally death, tries to separate us from God by breaking our links with him and severing our life-giving fellowship with him. But through the Cross, suffering has been humiliated. The suffering of Christ proves to be the grounds of our union with God, a union of sympathy which nothing can destroy. Suffering which was once seen as our enemy, something which separated us from God, can now be seen as something which can bring us closer to God.

Furthermore, we can rejoice in the sure and certain hope, grounded in the resurrection of Christ and sealed by the Holy Spirit, that one day we shall be delivered from the presence of suffering. There is a not-yet element to the victory of Christ over sin, death, and suffering. That hope can keep us going (and keep us growing!) in times of hardship.

The victory won over sin through the death of Christ is like the liberation of an occupied country. Try to imagine the mind-set of a citizen of an occupied European country such as France or Norway during the Second World War. Life has to be lived under the shadow of a foreign presence. And part of the poignancy of the situation is its apparent utter hopelessness. People think that nothing can be done about it.

Now imagine the electrifying news. There has been a far-off battle called D-Day that is turning the tide of the war. A new phase of the war is opening up, and the occupying power is in disarray. Its back has been broken. In the course of time the Nazis will be driven out of every corner of occupied Europe.

But the Nazis are still present in the occupied country. In one sense, the situation has not changed; but in another, more important sense, the situation has changed totally. The scent of victory and liberation is in the air. A total change in the psychological climate results.

I remember once meeting a man who had been held prisoner in the Japanese prisoner-of-war camp at Changi in Singapore. He told me of the astonishing change in the camp atmosphere which came about when one of the prisoners (who owned a short-wave radio) learned of the collapse of the Japanese war effort in the middle of 1945. Although all in the camp still remained prisoners, they knew that their enemy had been beaten. It was only a matter of time before they were to be released. Those prisoners, I was told, began to laugh and cry as if they were free, even though freedom had yet to come their way.

We remain captives in a world of suffering, as those prisoners remained incarcerated in that compound at Changi, yet the hope of liberation is at hand. The promise to be removed from imprisonment has been heard and has been made credible by the death and resurrection of Christ. We wait, but we wait in hope.

There is another aspect of Christ's victory over suffering. There is a day-to-day, moment-by-moment victory, which Christ died to make possible. Each time we suffer we are being offered an opportunity to claim a small victory over suffering by not allowing it to intimidate us and by not allowing it to succeed in breaking our trust in God. But more than that, we can allow God to speak to us through suffering as we shall see in the following chapter.

ELEVEN

Suffering and
Spiritual Growth

WHAT IS THE positive role of suffering in our lives? In a logical or philosophical sense, the fact of suffering is neutral. The important thing is what we make of it, both in terms of how we understand it, and in terms of how we allow it to affect us. Here is where theology helps; it allows us to see suffering in a positive light, as a means of growth rather than as something meaningless. We can learn to offer our sufferings and distress to God, assured that he can and will use them to bring us to new depths of faith and service.

We have already seen how God has the remarkable ability to work through suffering in ways which may not at first have been apparent. The cross of Christ must be our model here, reminding us of how God was able to take what to foolish human nature seemed to be a disastrous and pointless episode of anguish, and bring good from it. So are we just going to endure suffering, letting it wash over us? Are we going to pretend that this major experience is not going to change us in any way? Are we going to deny God the opportunity to speak to us through this experience? Or are we going to discern something potentially beneficial and helpful within it?

Someone who is determined not to see any meaning within suffering will not learn anything from the experience.

71

But someone who believes that God may be able to use suffering, to speak in it and through it, will be open to seeing the hand of God at work in this affliction. For Christians, God works through failure as much as through success, through suffering as much as through joy.

In an earlier chapter, we saw how suffering stripped away the delusions of security and immortality which seem to prevail outside the Christian faith. It peels away the veneer of assurance which can act as so powerful a barrier to the gospel. As a pastor, I have noticed how suffering can often be a way into the Christian faith. Often, the funeral of a partner proves to be a turning point in someone's spiritual journey, a time when the pieces of a complex puzzle suddenly fall into place. But it is not just those outside the Christian faith who can find their understanding of life transformed by suffering. It ought to be, above all, believers who grow through the experience of suffering. So how can Christians learn to understand how suffering can be handed over to God, with positive results? How can we grow through affliction?

In what follows, I shall explore a series of biblical images, each charged with enormous potential for understanding the positive role that suffering can play within the Christian life.

1. THE REFINER'S FIRE

The Old Testament often speaks of affliction or suffering in terms of the refining of faith. The imagery is powerful: in its crude state a precious metal, such as silver or gold, contains substantial amounts of impurities or "dross." The refiner's task is to remove this dross and, by doing so, to purify the metal, making it still more valuable. This is done by subjecting the metal to intense heat, for example, by passing it through a bed of white-hot coals. Suffering is seen as being like a refiner's fire, which removes the impurities from faith (e.g., Isa. 1:25; 48:10).

This way of thinking about the role of suffering in the Christian life has much to commend it. For example, only precious metals, like gold, were worth refining. Think of how precious our faith must be, if it is being refined by suffering (1 Peter 1:6–7). Realize how much more precious it will be, once all the dross has been removed.

Suffering gets rid of the dross of all the worldly supports we foolishly invent for our faith. Without realizing it, we often allow these supports to take the place of God. Suffering sets us on our own with God; it strips away our assurance and brings us face-to-face with God. With all the props of our faith stripped away, we learn to trust in God and lean upon him alone. Too often our faith rests on unreliable foundations such as satisfying personal relationships, a secure job, a healthy bank account, and physical health. Too easily these become God-substitutes. "Where your heart is, there is also your God" Luther wrote. Suffering or adversity strips them away and obliges us to discover God all over again. It brings us back to him by removing everything which we put in his place.

2. THE DISCIPLINE OF CHILDREN

Precisely because we are children of God by grace, we have the privilege of being disciplined by him: "the Lord disciplines those he loves" (Heb. 12:6; Prov. 3:11–12). Earlier, we spent some time reflecting about the nature of the love of God. That love is not something shallow and indulgent, which merely satisfies our fallen desires and short-term goals. The love of God is transformative, aiming to help us ultimately to achieve our chief end, which is "to glorify God and enjoy him forever" (Westminster Shorter Catechism). If the love of God is concerned to change us, to make us better, it must have the means available to do this. And one such means is discipline. Discipline enables us to keep hold of what we already possess of God, and to gain still more.

Jesus Christ was the Son of God who "learned obedience from what he suffered" (Heb. 5:8). As children of God, we share, by faith, in all that Christ gained and achieved. Just as he

73

suffered, so shall we suffer; just as he was glorified, so shall we be glorified. And just as he learned obedience through suffering, so must we learn obedience in the same way. It is a privilege which comes with being a child of God.

Discipline is a word that is too easily misunderstood. Too often, it conjures up images of unjustified punishment, of sadistic schoolmasters, and of the cruel and heartless atmosphere of Victorian boarding schools (so powerfully and shamefully described by Charles Dickens and others). But these are not the associations of the biblical term. Seen in its proper biblical context, discipline is nothing other than (and nothing less than) training for the race of faith. Just as Christ was made perfect through suffering (Heb. 5:8–9), so we who are united to him through faith must expect to share in his sufferings. Union with Christ through faith involves embracing the totality of Christ, not just those aspects that are easy to cope with! Suffering is integral, not optional, to those whose lives are, through the working of the Holy Spirit, being conformed to Christ.

But why do we need to be trained? A number of reasons come to mind. First, the Christian life is often compared to a battle. It is a struggle against sin, temptation, weakness, despair, confusion, and doubt. It helps in this struggle to know that God is on our side, that we have been well armed by the grace of God (Eph. 6:11–17), and that we are enabled ultimately to share in the victory which is ours through Christ. But the struggle goes on. If we are not to be overwhelmed, we must learn to be disciplined. A ragged and ill-disciplined army stands little chance against a determined opponent.

God has already given us much to enable us to survive, indeed, even to prosper, in this combat. Discipline is a developed ability to cope with difficult situations, which is acquired through training and exposure to the sort of difficulties that lie ahead. Suffering and affliction hone our defenses and strengthen our resolve to fight on against all the forces ranged against us which attempt to drag us back into the dusk of unbelief and lostness.

3. THE PRUNING OF A PLANT

Christians are like branches on a vine (John 15:1–11). The image has many aspects. For example, we learn that unless a branch remains firmly attached to the stem of the vine, it will wither and die, and cease to bear fruit (15:4–6). The life-giving sap must be able to get through to the branch, if it is to grow and be fruitful. And so Christians must abide in Christ, remaining close to him and nestling in his presence, if they are to grow in grace and bear fruit in their lives. If a branch becomes detached from the vine, it will shrivel and wilt and become like any other piece of dead wood, fit only for throwing away. Christians who wander from the nourishing and sustaining presence of Christ will end up withering in their faith, and losing their distinctiveness.

Now the vine grower is aware of how useless such branches are. If a branch does not bear any fruit, he will remove it. But what happens to branches that bear fruit? Does the vine grower leave them alone? No. In order to encourage and enable them to bear more fruit, he prunes them (15:2). Pruning is a tribute to the potential of a branch. It is an acknowledgment that it is already fruitful, and a recognition of its even greater capacity to bear fruit in the future. Pruning is not just a mark of favor; it is a mark of expectation and anticipation on the part of the vine owner.

Suffering is like pruning. It is cutting off spurious growths which might be of no value or stopping shoots which, were they to grow further, would weaken the vine. It hurts the branch to be pruned. When you prune a rose, a fruit tree, or a vine, you can see the wounds that you are inflicting upon it. But your pruning is not arbitrary, pointless, and vindictive infliction of suffering upon an innocent and unsuspecting plant! It is an action designed to inflict the minimum of damage upon the plant, while at the same time achieving maximum enhancement of its potential. Those who suffer may well be those who bear the most effective witness and thus those who bear the most fruit in and through their Christian lives.

75

4. THE HUMILITY OF FAITH

The word *humility* comes from the Latin word *humus,* meaning "earth." To be humbled is to be brought down to earth, to be reminded of our lowly origins.

Humility is a recognition that all we have, and all that we are, is a gift from God. Our gifts, talents, and achievements are not something that we own or possess. They are not even things which we accomplish unaided. Rather, they are gracious gifts from God, an expression of the generosity of God, not of our deserving or merits. Humility does not deny that we have gifts or talents, but is an unpretentious willingness to admit that everything we have and everything that we are is the result of the grace of God, not only our efforts or achievements.

By recognizing that all our resources for the Christian life come from God, we are enabled to avoid two of the worst pitfalls that occur in the Christian life. First, we begin to succumb to the attractive illusion that we can cope by ourselves. And by doing so, we cut ourselves off from the lifeline offered by God. If we think that we can look after ourselves, we don't bother looking anywhere else for support. Second, we become spiritually proud. We begin to think of things in terms of our achievements, our gifts, our talents, and so on. We lose sight of the fact that they are God's gifts, and that we are their stewards, not their owners. Our task is to make the best possible use of them, before returning them to their owner. (The parable of the talents in Matthew 25:14–30 makes this point superbly.)

Suffering humbles us. It reminds us that we do not have full control over our own situation. This is especially well illustrated in the life of the Swiss reformer Ulrich Zwingli. A pastor at Zurich in 1519, when the city was struck by an outbreak of the plague, Zwingli visited the sick regularly and soon contracted the disease himself. As he lay on his sickbed, he realized that whether he lived or died was totally beyond his control. He was powerless. "Make what you will of me!" was his prayer. In the end, Zwingli recovered, but his spirituality henceforth resonates with the theme of humility. It is God who achieves things for us and who always offers to achieve more. Through his suffering, with all its attendant anxiety and uncertainty, Zwingli learned to look towards God for his security.

Suffering often brings home to us how powerless and helpless we are in the face of illness and death. A colleague of mine had become very old and ill and was close to death. When I went to see him, he was quite happy to talk about his illness and what its eventual outcome would be. I was enormously impressed by his courage and found myself wondering if I would be able to match it when my turn came. But what I remember most clearly from that discussion was the effect that his debilitating illness had upon his understanding of grace.

"I can't do anything for myself now. I have to rely totally on the kindness of others." He paused. "The grace of God has come to mean far more to me now than it ever did before. It's like someone kind helping a helpless old man like me." In his utter helplessness, the idea of grace had assumed a new reality and meaning. The idea had come to life for him. Grace wasn't just a word anymore. It was something on which his existence depended. His reflections on his own predicament, brought about by his illness, brought new depth to one of the most familiar words of the gospel vocabulary.

5. THE WITNESS OF SUFFERING

Some of Paul's finest writing has its origin in his captivity at Rome—possibly in prison, probably in some form of protective custody. On account of his having preached the gospel faithfully, Paul was "suffering even to the point of being chained like a criminal" (2 Tim. 2:9). While taking comfort that the gospel itself could not be bound and imprisoned in this way, it is clear that Paul was distressed by the experience.

Yet his affliction gave him new opportunities to witness to those around him. "What has happened to me has really served to advance the gospel" (Phil. 1:12). Everyone knew that he had been imprisoned on account of his faith in Christ, so this provided him with a series of new opportunities to proclaim Christ. The point to be made is simple: in whatever situation we find ourselves, we are able to witness to the love of God in Christ.

Faith is something which affects our entire outlook on life, including the way in which we cope with pain and affliction. Suffering is often a public event. Other people often notice the way in which we react to hardship, illness, suffering, and dying. I used to work as a pastor in Nottingham in England's east Midlands. Part of my job was to officiate at funerals. As a result, I got to know most of the staff at the city's various funeral homes. They often talked about their work. One of the things that they found most difficult was the first visit to the home of the surviving relatives of the person who had died. Sometimes it was a harrowing experience, at others, it was not. "You can usually tell fairly quickly whether they are religious or not," one commented (to general assent). "They seem so calm and peaceful, where anyone else would have been having hysterics."

Suffering does not prevent us from affirming our faith and trust in God; it may indeed open up new ways of doing so. The Christian church has always recognized that dying, as well as living, provides believers with opportunities to declare their faith to the world. The North African Christian theologian Tertullian, writing in the early third century, remarked that "the blood of the martyrs is the seed of the church."

We have considered five possible ways in which suffering can be understood within the context of the Christian life. Suffering is a valuable and potentially productive aspect of the Christian life which leads to Christian maturity and the full stature of discipleship. But it must be seen in the right light before its maturing potential can be realized.

TWELVE

Sharing in the Suffering of Christ

I consider everything a loss compared to the surpassing greatness of knowing Christ Jesus my Lord, for whose sake I have lost all things . . . I want to know Christ and the power of his resurrection and the fellowship of sharing in his sufferings, becoming like him in his death" (Phil. 3:8–10). Read these words and savor them, turning them over in your mind as they cast light on the place of suffering in the Christian life.

We could sum up much of what Paul is describing here by saying that the Christian life is *Christomorphic*. This, like many other words in the theologian's vocabulary, is a clumsy term. Yet its outward ugliness conceals an inner sweetness. For it expresses the idea that faith "shapes us in the form of Christ." Through faith, God breaks us and remolds us, casting us in the shape of his own Son. The pattern of the life of Christ begins to make itself evident in our own lives as we begin to live in ways that express his compassion and care, in the quiet confidence that we shall one day share also in his risen glory.

But there is a darker side to this. We who are being made like Christ must expect to share in his sufferings before we share in his glory. Suffering and pain may seem utterly pointless and meaningless, but then Christ's death on the cross seemed much the same. One of the most wonderful insights of the gospel is that God is able to transfigure suffering, which seems to have no meaning and no purpose, and achieve something through it. We may not know what is being achieved—after all, those watching Christ die had no inkling of the amazing events which were to follow in its wake. It may seem to us, too, that our pain and hurt serve no purpose. But that feeling unites us to Christ in his pain and sorrow at Calvary. The same God who brought purpose and power out of the seemingly meaningless sufferings of his Son is present, through faith, in our sufferings today. We must learn to offer them to him, and ask him to reassure us of his presence, power, and purpose in our own little scenes of crucifixion. So important is this theme of suffering with Christ that we will consider it in more detail in what follows.

The New Testament is permeated with the theme of suffering—both the sufferings of Christ on the cross and the sufferings of his people as they bear witness to him. To be a Christian is to suffer. Christianity thus openly acknowledges the reality and the pain of suffering. Not for one moment is there a suggestion that someone, by becoming a Christian, can evade or escape from the world of suffering. Christians may not be of the world; they nevertheless remain in the world. There is no way in which coming to faith involves being isolated from the suffering of the world.

Christians are in the world because they are meant to be in that world. There is no insulation, no cushioning from the harsh realities of life. The hope of heaven is real, but it does not shield us from the pain of this present life. The suffering, crucifixion, and resurrection of Jesus Christ map out the shape of the true Christian life. The only road that leads to hope passes through suffering and death. From the perspective of the Road, other routes may seem easier and more attractive, but from the Balcony they are seen to be dead ends.

To become a real Christian may also involve entering into suffering on account of faith itself. "Christ suffered for you, leaving you an example, that you should follow in his steps" (1 Peter 2:21). It is to take up a cross and follow Christ. Suffer-

ing is part of the lot of the believer. "Rejoice that you participate in the sufferings of Christ, so that you may be overjoyed
when his glory is revealed" (1 Peter 4:13).

So does this mean that Christians should seek out suffering, so that they can be more like Christ? No. Suffering comes
our way in God's own good time, if it comes at all. The time
and place of suffering are best left to the wisdom of God. What
matters is how we view that suffering and how we are prepared to use it.

Some, like Job's misguided comforters, will always insist
that suffering is a mark of divine disfavor or punishment. But
responsible Christian theology knows otherwise. From the
Road, suffering looks like unequivocally bad news. It seems to
show that we are cut off from the presence of God. But from the
Balcony, things look different. Suffering is seen as a potential
mark of God's favor and presence, as he allows us the privilege
in sharing in the suffering of his own Son. Suffering is the same
experience, whether viewed from the Balcony or the Road, but
it is seen in a very different light and with equally different
results. Those on the Road need the perspective of the Balconeers if they are to cope with suffering and to learn from it.

Suffering does not mean that we are far from God; it can
mean that we are being drawn closer to him, and are being
allowed to go through an experience that can break down the
remaining barriers between ourselves and him. It was through
the bitter experience of a "thorn in the flesh" that Paul learned
that most important spiritual lesson—that the grace of God
was sufficient for him, and that the power of God is made perfect in human weakness (2 Cor. 12:7–10). As Martin Luther
emphasized many times, suffering is a tool by which God can
strip away our veneer of self-satisfaction and self-delusion and
help us to face up to our weakness and his strength.

But if the gospel means only suffering, in what sense is it
good news? The Christian answer to this question is powerful
and needs to be heard carefully. Through faith, we are caught
up in the life of Christ. We become united with Christ and

81

share in all that he is and achieves. A number of images are used within the Christian tradition to bring out the full richness of this theme: for example, the legal images of adoption and marriage.

The image of *adoption* is used by Paul to express the relation between believers and Jesus Christ (Rom. 8:15; 8:23; 9:4; Gal. 4:5; Eph. 1:5). Under Roman law, a father could adopt people from outside his natural family and give them the status of family members. Although a distinction would still be possible between the natural and adopted children, they had the same legal status. In the eyes of the law, they were all members of the same family irrespective of their origins.

Paul deploys the adoption image partly to indicate that faith brings about a change in our status before God, incorporating us within the family of God, despite the fact that we do not share the same divine origins as Christ. But he also makes use of the idea in another manner. To be an adopted child is to share the same inheritance rights as the natural children. As believers, we thus inherit from God our Father, in much the same way as Christ does. We are heirs of God, and co-heirs with Christ. And what does this mean? It means that we can, in due course, expect to inherit everything that Christ received as an inheritance from God. And what did Christ receive? According to Paul, in the first place suffering, and in the second, glory. No suffering, no glory. Through faith, we come to share in this pattern of divine inheritance mapped out for us by Christ: suffering, followed by glory (Rom. 8:17; 1 Peter 3:12–14).

A second image is that of *marriage,* hinted at by Paul, and, as we shall see, developed in the writings of such thinkers as Martin Luther and John Calvin. Faith is like a marriage bond. It unites two people in a real and personal union. To be a Christian is to be in Christ—that is, to be united through faith to the risen Christ. In marriage, a man and a woman come together in a union which involves the mutual sharing of goods. What belongs to the groom is shared with the bride, just as what belongs to the bride is shared with the groom.

82

To think of faith as a marriage between the believer and Christ thus emphasizes the real and personal nature of the union between them. Faith is not knowing *about* Christ; it is *knowing* Christ, and being known by him. Faith is not about theories or ideas. It is about personal relationships that transform us and about a real sharing between the believer and Christ. But it is an unequal sharing. We give Christ our sins and mortality. He bestows upon us his righteousness and grace—and his earthly suffering and heavenly glorification. These become ours through faith. Every now and then, our pain may be transfigured by glimpses of his glory.

Suffering is part of a greater whole. It is the link between our present state of lowliness and our future state of glory. Theology allows us to see suffering as a window into the presence of God. We see through it and beyond it, and catch a glimpse of the glory and presence of God which lies through its gateway. It cannot be avoided, but it need not be feared.

The idea that to become a Christian is to enter the experience of the suffering people of God, who are able to witness to God through that suffering and draw nearer to him as a result of it pervades the New Testament. Perhaps the most moving statement of this belief can be found in 1 Peter. Christians are those who have been called "out of darkness into God's wonderful light" (2:9). Yet the world resents their presence and their calling and inflicts suffering upon them as a result. "Dear friends, do not be surprised at the painful trial you are suffering, as though something strange were happening to you. But rejoice that you participate in the sufferings of Christ, so that you may be overjoyed when his glory is revealed" (4:12–13). Suffering is not a sign of being outside the family of God, but a distinguishing mark of membership.

So to be united to Christ is to share in his sufferings and to hope to share in his risen glory. To *hope* to share? Yes. Faith is about being able to see beyond the present life to that which lies thereafter. Present suffering will give way to future glory, as surely as Good Friday gave way to Easter Day. To those outside the Christian faith, who refuse to believe in anything beyond the present order of things, suffering can only be seen as an end. It has no possibility of being transformed. But the Christian knows of the transfiguration of suffering through resurrection, and so lives in hope. We shall explore this theme in our final chapter.

THIRTEEN

The Hope of Glory

SUFFERING AND DEATH, like sin, are hateful to God. Jesus wept as he stood before the tomb of Lazarus. The same Jesus who is none other than Immanuel, God with us, cried over the death of one of his creatures, whom he loved. The tears of Christ are a powerful reminder of the compassion of God as we, like Lazarus, suffer and die.

John paints the most tender picture of Jesus, deeply affected by the grief of Mary and Martha. I have often wondered how best to translate the Greek text of John 11:33. Jesus is deeply moved; he is greatly upset; he is perhaps even angry. About what? About the pain of the human situation, and the grief that it occasions. Suffering, death, and sin are all part of our tragic fallen human situation. It is important to affirm the Christian belief that the way things are is not the way things are meant to be, nor the way they shall remain.

Some say that nothing could ever be adequate recompense for the suffering in this world. But how do they know? Have they spoken to anyone who has suffered and subsequently been raised to glory? Have they been through this experience themselves? Paul believed passionately that the sufferings of the present life would be outweighed by the glory that is to come (Rom. 8:18). How do they know that he is wrong, and that they are right?

If we could listen to someone who had suffered a humiliating and painful death, and then returned to us from the dead, he would speak with authority and insight on this matter. It is here that the resurrection of Christ becomes of central importance. God has indeed spoken on such matters. We can know something of what lies ahead. We can see suffering from the perspective of eternity.

At the time of Christ, people expected a general resurrection at the end of time. It would mark the end of history and was to be accompanied by divine judgment and the self-revelation of God. The resurrection of Christ was thus totally unexpected. It didn't fit any of the expected patterns of the time. It was as if something that was meant to happen at the end of time had taken place right in the middle of human history.

The resurrection thus allows the suffering of Christ to be seen from the perspective of eternity. Suffering is not pointless, but leads to glory. Those who share in the sufferings of Christ may, through the resurrection of Christ, know what awaits them at the end of history. It is for this reason that Paul is able to declare with such confidence that "our present sufferings are not worth comparing with the glory that will be revealed in us" (Rom. 8:18). This is no groundless hope, no arbitrary aspiration. It is a hard-headed realism, grounded in the reality of the suffering and resurrection of Christ and the knowledge that faith binds us to Christ and guarantees that we shall share in his heritage.

The New Testament affirms that the sufferings of this earth are real and painful. God is deeply pained by our suffering, just as we are shocked, grieved, and mystified by the suffering of our family and friends. But that is only half of the story. The other half must be told. It is natural that our attention should be fixed upon what we experience and feel here and now. But faith demands that we raise our sights and look to what lies ahead. We may suffer as we journey, but where are we going? What lies ahead?

The word *heaven* seems inadequate to describe the final goal of faith. Perhaps we should speak more expansively of the hope of eternal life, of the renewing of our frail and mortal bodies in the likeness of Christ's glorious resurrection body, and of the ultimate prize of standing, redeemed, in the presence of God. But however we choose to describe it, the promise and hope of our transformation and renewal and of the transfiguration of suffering are an integral part of the Christian faith. This glorious thread is woven so deeply into the fabric of our faith that it cannot possibly be removed.

The language of prizes and rewards is helpful in many ways. It reminds us of the need to complete the race in order that we may receive the athlete's crown (2 Tim. 4:7–8). It reminds us of the need for training and discipline in the Christian life, to build up the stamina we need in order to persevere.

But this way of thinking about the relation between suffering and heaven can also be misleading. It implies an accidental connection between suffering and heaven. It suggests that heaven is thrown in as some kind of consolation prize, in order to keep us going here below. In his acclaimed sermon "The Weight of Glory," C. S. Lewis addressed this question as follows:

> There are different kinds of reward. There is the reward which has no natural connection with the things you do to earn it, and is quite foreign to the desires that ought to accompany those things. Money is not the natural reward of love; that is why we call a man mercenary if he marries a woman for the sake of her money. But marriage is the proper reward for a real lover, and he is not mercenary for desiring it. … The proper rewards are not simply tacked on to the activities for which they are given, but are the activity itself in consummation.

The danger identified by Lewis is easily avoided if we pay more attention to the intimacy of the connection between suffering and glory.

When a seed is planted in the ground, it begins to grow and will eventually bear fruit. Can we say that its bearing fruit is a reward for its growth? No. We would say that there is an organic and natural connection between one and the other. That is just the way things are. It is not a question of declaring, in some arbitrary way, that a seed which grows will be rewarded with fruit, or that the prize for growth is fruit. Rather, we view germination, growth, and the bearing of fruit as all part of the same overall process. They are all stages in the natural cycle of growth and development.

And so with suffering and glorification. They are part of, but represent different stages in the process of growth in the Christian life. We are adopted into the family of God, we suffer, and we are glorified (Rom. 8:15–18). This is not an accidental relationship. Each step is intimately connected within the overall pattern of Christian growth and progress toward the ultimate goal of the Christian life—being finally united with God and remaining with him forever. Heaven is the consummation of a process of which suffering is a present part.

We are thus presented with a glorious vision of a new realm of existence. It is a realm in which suffering has been defeated. It is a realm pervaded by the refreshing presence of God, from which the presence and power of sin have finally been excluded. It lies ahead, and we have yet to enter into it, even if we can catch a hint of its fragrance and hear its music in the distance. It is this hope which keeps us going in this life of sadness, which ends in death.

But is it for real? Is this hope anything more than wishful thinking, a spurious pipe dream, a pitiful hope on the part of human beings who long for a better world than that which they now know and inhabit? We are all familiar with the tedious taunt of believing in "pie in the sky when you die." The implication seems to be that Christians are so deluded and unrealistic about life that they need such fictional morsels to keep them going, whereas others can cope with the grim realities of life unaided.

But this evades the question. Is it true? If it is true, Christians can hardly be criticized for believing in it. If it is true, to ignore it is to run away from reality. Either it is true, or it is not. So which is it? Let us be absolutely clear on this. If the Christian hope of heaven is an illusion, based upon lies, then it must be abandoned as misleading and deceitful. But if it is true, it must be embraced and allowed to transfigure our entire understanding of the place of suffering in life.

I believe it is for real, and that it is impossible for a Christian to discuss suffering without reference to it. Through the grace of God, suffering gives way to glory, as a woman's pain in childbirth gives way to the joy of new birth.

The Christian hope of heaven is deeply embedded within the gospel. It is not some add-on feature, some optional extra which got tacked on to the gospel at a later stage, and which can be discarded at will. As I stressed earlier, it is part of an overall pattern of growth and development, comparable to the germination of a seed, leading to the growth and final coming to fruit of the resulting plant.

The most helpful analogy for understanding this vital point is that of a human marriage, with faith being seen as analogous to the marriage bond uniting husband and wife. Martin Luther stated this principle in his 1520 writing, *The Liberty of a Christian*:

> Faith unites the soul with Christ as a bride is united with her bridegroom. As Paul teaches us, Christ and the soul become one flesh by this mystery (Ephesians 5:31–2). And if they are one flesh, and if the marriage is for real ... then it follows that everything that they have is held in common, whether good or evil. So the believer can boast of and glory in whatever Christ possesses, as though it were his or her own. And whatever the believer has, Christ claims as his own. Let us see how this works out, and see how it benefits us. Christ is full of grace, life and salvation. The human soul is full of sin, death and damnation. Now let faith come between them. Sin, death and damnation will be Christ's. And grace, life and salvation will be the believer's.

A human marriage is no legal fiction. It is a real and vital relationship between two persons, involving personal union, mutual commitment, a common life, and a sharing of goods.

Precisely this relationship is established between the believer and the risen Christ through faith.

The believer thus comes to be "in Christ." He or she is a new creation. A dynamic bond is forged between the believing human being and the redeeming Christ, bringing in its wake a partaking of all that he won for us by his obedience. But whereas death eventually parts a human couple, nothing—not even death itself—can destroy the union between Christ and the believer. It is for real, and it is forever. Indeed, death merely snaps the final surly bonds which link us with the unredeemed world of sin, enabling us to commit ourselves totally and unreservedly to Christ.

The believer thus shares in Christ's victory over death, his breaking free from the bonds of suffering and pain, and his risen life. Christians are assured that they will share in this resurrection, and will share the life of the risen, ascended and glorified Christ. The victory over sin is only complete when we are saved, not merely from its penalty and power, but also from its presence. Here the great promises of the Old Testament find their final fulfillment. We are brought into the presence of God, rejoicing.

This, then, is the hope of faith. Hope! How much spiritual excitement and depth is compressed into that single word. This is no shallow optimism, no vague and unformed wish that all might turn out well, when everything indicates it will not. "I hope that George won't make a fool of himself again tonight." "I hope it will stop raining soon." No. Here is a sure and confident expectation, born of the trustworthiness of God, nourished by his promises, and sustained by the gracious working of the Holy Spirit.

This sure anticipation of our future union with God allows us to yearn passionately to be with God, to crave for his closer presence, and to view this life in the light of this final goal. Just as a soldier fights on towards the end of a long war, sustained by the knowledge that peace will one day come and he will be reunited with his family and friends, so the Christian continues his pilgrimage, sustained by the knowledge of the joys that await him.

Karl Marx regarded this outlook on life as little more than nauseating sentimentality. By offering us hope for the future, he thought it distracted us from changing the world for the better. To use Marx's famous phrase, Christianity is "an opiate for the masses," a kind of anesthetic or narcotic which dulls our senses and prevents us from doing something about the shameful situation of our world.

Now Marx has a fair point. So great is the attractiveness of the Christian hope that it is natural to become fascinated by it and to want to focus our thoughts upon it. It is all too easy to become so heavenly minded as to be of no earthly use. If Marx's criticism serves any useful purpose, it is to remind us that we have a Christian duty to work for the transformation of the world as we know it by removing the causes of unnecessary suffering. The Christian hope ought to be a stimulus, rather than a sedative. It should spur us to action within the world, rather than encourage us to neglect it. By working to lessen the suffering of God's world and his people, we are easing his heartache over their pain.

But when all is said and done, Marx's comment merely reinforces the power and importance of the Christian hope. The fact that it does enable us to cope with suffering in the present life is at the same time both its danger and its attractiveness. Precisely because it so successfully enables us to cope with the turmoil and sorrow of the world, it could tempt us to leave them unaltered. Marx is thus a reluctant, yet eloquent witness to the power of the Christian hope to enable us to cope with the dark side of life.

So how does this hope console us? By setting our present situation in its full context. By allowing eternity to break into time and illuminate it. By reminding and reassuring us that "our present sufferings are not worth comparing with the glory that will be revealed in us" (Rom. 8:18). By calling to our memory those great figures of the past who, by faith, reached out to receive the same hope, without the benefit of the firm assurances given to us through Christ that these promises would find their fulfillment (Heb. 11:1–40).

Are we frightened by death? Faith assures us that to die is to gain, and to be with the Christ we long to know fully. Are we troubled by sorrow? Faith tells us of another country where sorrow is no more and where all tears have been wiped away. Do we suffer? Faith tells us of a time when death shall be swallowed up in victory and the sufferings of the present day will seem insignificant in comparison with the joy that awaits us. And how great those sufferings are for so many. Is it not consoling to trust that the bliss of heaven will exceed them both in intensity and duration?

Just as suffering is real, so are the promises of God and the hope of eternal life. The death and resurrection of Christ, linked with the giving of the Holy Spirit, are pledges, sureties, and guarantees that what has been promised will one day be brought to glorious realization. For the moment we struggle and suffer in sadness mingled with bewilderment. But one day, all that will be changed for the people of God:

> God himself will be with them and be their God. He will wipe every tear from their eyes. There will be no more death or mourning or crying or pain, for the old order of things has passed away (Rev. 21:3–4).

In that hope we go forward into life in faith. We may not know exactly where that faith will lead us. But we do know that wherever we go, the God of all compassion goes ahead of us and journeys with us, consoling and reassuring us, until that day when we shall see him face-to-face and know him as he knows us.